Celebrating Language With Adult Literacy Students
Lessons to Engage and Inspire

Francis E. Kazemek

INTERNATIONAL
Reading Association
800 BARKSDALE ROAD, PO BOX 8139
NEWARK, DE 19714-8139, USA
www.reading.org

The International Reading Association attempts, through
its publications, to provide a forum for a wide spectrum
of opinions on reading. This policy permits divergent
viewpoints without implying the endorsement
of the Association.

Executive Editor, Books	Corinne M. Mooney
Developmental Editor	Charlene M. Nichols
Developmental Editor	Tori Mello Bachman
Developmental Editor	Stacey Lynn Sharp
Editorial Production Manager	Shannon T. Fortner
Design and Composition Manager	Anette Schuetz
Project Editors	Charlene M. Nichols and Rebecca A. Stewart
Cover	design by SR NOVA

The publisher would appreciate notification where errors
occur so that they may be corrected in subsequent
printings and/or editions.

Library of Congress Cataloging-in-Publication Data
Kazemek, Francis E.
Celebrating language with adult literacy students:
lessons to engage and inspire / Francis E. Kazemek.
p. cm.
Includes bibliographical references and index.
ISBN 978-0-87207-685-3
1. Functional literacy--United States. 2. English
language--Writing--Study and teaching. I. Title.
LC151.K388 2008
374'.012--dc22
2008025111

For Cheryl, with love.
In memory of my Mom and Dad, who with limited education
were my first models of how to be literate in the world.

Contents

About the Author

FRANCIS E. KAZEMEK is a Professor of Education at St. Cloud State University in Minnesota, USA. He has taught elementary through university-level students and has been involved in adult literacy education for the past 25 years. Francis was a faculty exchange professor at Odessa State University in Ukraine and at Cape Coast University in Ghana. During the 1999–2000 academic year he was a Fulbright Scholar to Norway where he conducted American Studies classes and writing workshops for teachers and high school students.

Francis's scores of academic articles on aspects of literacy/literature education in general and adult literacy in particular have appeared in many professional journals, and his coauthored book *Enriching Our Lives: Poetry Lessons for Adult Literacy Teachers and Tutors* was published by the International Reading Association. His recent book, *Exploring Our Lives: A Writing Handbook for Senior Adults*, was published by Santa Monica Press. Francis's poetry and short stories have appeared in various magazines and journals.

Francis began conducting writing workshops for elders in 1981 and continues to do so in a number of locations. In recent years he has developed oral history and other projects that foster intergenerational storytelling and writing between school children and adults. He writes weekly with adolescents in alternative learning centers and regularly with adults in a variety of contexts. The value of poetry for people of all ages and its importance in helping individuals become critical and creative thinkers, readers, and writers is one of his ruling passions. For questions or comments, Francis can be reached at kazemek@bwig.net.

Introduction

WHY DO WE WRITE? Why do we encourage others to write? When we speak of literacy in the 21st century, are more expansive forms of writing any longer of much importance? Shouldn't we be more concerned with helping people become skilled with e-mail and text messaging, with their various forms of shorthand, freedom from punctuation and grammar, and emphasis on functionality? It is getting difficult to find individuals who still communicate by personal letters through the mail, so why waste time and effort on exploring such personal writing? Even among close friends and family members, written communication in the form of e-mails reflects what we typically see in workplace writing: functional texts that are brief and information based.

So why do we write and help others learn to write? The poet–farmer Wendell Berry explains the *necessity* of writing that is more than functional:

> I would not have been a poet
> except that I have been in love
> alive in this mortal world,
> or an essayist except that I
> have been bewildered and afraid,
> or a storyteller had I not heard
> stories passing to me through the air
> or a writer at all except
> I have been wakeful at night
> and words have come to me
> out of their deep caves
> needing to be remembered.

> (Berry, 1998, p. 182) Copyright 1999 by Wendell Berry from *A Timbered Choir: The Sabbath Poems 1979–1997*. Reprinted by permission of the publisher.

We write because we love people, places, things, beauty, memories, and dreams of the future. Writing can be an act of love and a means of paying tribute to it. We write as a means of exploring ideas, fears, contradictions, and confusions. Writing can

1

help us clarify what we think and believe. We write because we want to capture in a more permanent form the stories of our lives and those of others. Writing can help us, as storytelling creatures, affirm our humanity. Writing can help us embrace the words and images welling up inside us in our most contemplative moments. We write because we have to.

I do not suggest that all writing should be of this expansive nature. By expansive I mean writing that helps us review and re-vision (i.e., see again) our lives and not simply get lost in our daily living, and therefore writing that is reflective and necessary. As the imaginal psychologist James Hillman (1999) observes, we don't really "know" ourselves as we go through life; rather, we "discover" ourselves, and such writing helps us on our journey of discovery. There certainly is a place and a necessity for functional writing, whether in the workplace or in a text message that tells a friend you'll meet her at a restaurant around noon. However, without poems, stories, vignettes—imaginative patterns of some sort—there is only news and limited understanding (Kazemek, 1991, 1999b).

This book is about writing that is more than news, more than functional, basic, or workplace literacy. It is for those literacy educators and volunteer tutors who are eager to write with their students as a means of celebrating language and honoring their own and their students' lives. It is for those adult educators who realize that they are struggling in an era of conservative reductionism, a time in which, as George Demetrion (2005) has observed, business metaphors abound and "performance-based accountability premised on the quest for comparability through measurable, uniform, and objective standards" holds sway (p. 107). The discussions, examples, suggestions, lessons, strategies, and recommended texts found in this book are based on my quarter century of writing with people of all ages, from 8 to 92. I particularly highlight what I have learned by working with adults who were less proficient in reading and writing than they wanted to be. Often what I learned by writing with such adults was more than I ever did in formal school or academic settings.

Perspective

Education

Those of us working with adult new or developing readers and writers have an underlying educational philosophy and theory of literacy. Generally, however, our particular theories and philosophies are seldom consciously articulated. Indeed, we might sometimes engage in practices and use materials that are in conflict with or even antithetical to what we believe. Thus, I want to state clearly the views that serve as the basis of this book.

I believe that the purpose of education at all levels from kindergarten through adulthood is not only to help us become knowledgeable and skilled in particular disciplines but also to help us become more critical, reflective, and empathetic human beings who are able to engage the world from multiple perspectives. We do this by actively exploring topics with others and not by listening to "experts" talk at us. As the passionate adult literacy educator Paulo Freire maintained, we read the word by reading the world and not by having someone "bank" information in our heads. Thus, education for adults should promote wide reading; varieties of writing; viewing and listening to various media; and using technology to help individuals analyze, discuss, and debate various aesthetic, political, philosophical, psychological, and sociological perspectives. It should highlight the wealth of diversity and also the commonalties that exist among all people, for example, the need for community, love, and a sense of competence and worth.

Of course education might have more limited objectives at times. Adults might want or need to learn specific things for the workplace. They might memorize facts or procedures in order to pass different tests. They might orally drill again and again with words and phrases in order to become fluent in their new language. All of these practices certainly have their place. However, if they aren't embedded within a much larger, humane, and moral educational context then they become little more than training exercises, and we know that there is a difference between training and education. The etymological roots of the verb *train* emphasize drawing or dragging forth, while those of *educate* highlight leading forth. Adult education should be about leading others—and ourselves—in new and richer directions.

Literacy

Literacy is a complex web of functional and social practices that involve the active engagement of the four language modes, that is, listening, speaking, reading, and writing. It involves the individual within her particular social and economic context (I vary gender references throughout the book). In her study of literacy in the United States over the past century, Deborah Brandt (2001) has explored the connection between literacy as an individual development and literacy as an economic development by highlighting what she calls the "sponsors of literacy":

> Sponsors, as I have come to think of them, are any agents, local or distant, concrete or abstract, who enable, support, teach, and model, as well as recruit, regulate, suppress, or withhold literacy—and gain advantage by it in some way. (p. 19)

Thus, it is hard to think honestly of literacy as some simple process by which an isolated individual learns his letters, sounds, and words through decontextualized workbook practice:

> It's easy to treat literacy as some packaged commodity unconnected to individual passions and the economic and social demands of the contexts in which adults find themselves. However, such approaches to adult literacy education are ultimately of small value. (Kazemek, 2004, p. 451)

Indeed, literacy is not singular but rather plural. There are really *literacies* and not simply some universal practice in which all people engage. These literacies are different sets of social practices that vary according to different personal needs and interests, or as David Barton and Mary Hamilton (1998) point out, a person's "ruling passion" or particular desire in life (p. 18). Moreover, literacies are often processes of informal and vernacular usage and are embedded within webs of language use, media, and technology. As Louise Rosenblatt (1978) points out, "A specific reader and a specific text at a specific time and place: change any of these, and there occurs a different circuit, a different event—a different poem [refers to the whole category of literary works]" (p. 14).

I am concerned primarily with *print literacy* as defined by Victoria Purcell-Gates, Erik Jacobson, and Sophie Degener (2004):

> Print literacy is the reading and writing of some form of print for communicative purposes inherent in peoples' lives. Thus, it involves decoding and encoding of a linguistically based symbol system and is driven by social processes that rely upon communication and meaning. Because it is social, its practice reflects sociocultural patterns and purposes as well as power relationships and political forces. (p. 26)

Accordingly, my purpose in this book is to approach adult literacy (literacies) education through the writing and reading of many different kinds of texts and through the play of different forms of language.

As my theoretical touchstone I am using the work of the writing scholar and researcher James Britton (1982). Britton says that we can think of different kinds of writing as places along a continuum. At one end of the continuum is what he calls "transactional" or functional writing, and at the other is "poetic" writing. In the middle is "expressive" writing. Transactional writing is what we do to get things done, for example, grocery lists, notes on the refrigerator for family members, letters of excuse to teachers for a child's absence, business letters, recipes, e-mail requests for information, and so forth. When we do this kind of writing Britton says that we are acting in the role of a "participant," that is, we are actively engaged with the world through the writing. We might think of this kind of writing as a functional tool. We are less concerned with elegance and sometimes pay less attention to spelling, grammar, and punctuation. Think of the grocery lists we scribble before we go to the supermarket or the sticky note we place on the freezer door: "Do NOT eat the icecream!!!!"

Poetic writing, on the other hand, is concerned with elegance, word choice, and the construction of something special with language. Poetic writing of course includes poetry, but it is more than that. With this kind of writing we are concerned with making something beautiful, and in doing so we take on the role of a "spectator." We are not actively engaged in getting something done in the world, as we are with transactional writing, but instead we are able to step back and look at how our language works and how we are creating something unique. Poetic writing includes such things as stories, novels, drama, tall tales, song lyrics, jokes, and riddles. It emphasizes the made work of art.

Between transactional and poetic is what James Britton (1982) calls expressive writing, and this is the writing that is closest to ourselves. It expresses who we are, how we feel and think about things, and often reveals our deepest fears, joys, loves, and hates. Expressive writing includes such things as personal journals, private diaries, and prayers. Britton contends that all writing of whatever nature should first be grounded in the expressive. This is especially true for adult new readers and writers who typically have had little opportunity to explore and express themselves through writing.

It is important not to simplify these three types of writing and try to rigidly employ James Britton's scheme. Any piece of writing might reflect two or even all three types depending upon the writer's purpose and his audience. Think, for example, of a person writing a letter to the manufacturer of a shoddy product that was purchased online through the Internet. His ultimate purpose is to get a refund, and thus he is engaging in transactional writing. However, he is also very angry at being duped and wants to convey his outrage; in doing so he is engaging in expressive writing. Moreover, he wants to do all of this through a well-constructed piece of satire. He chooses his words carefully, makes ironic allusions, and engages in black humor. By doing so he is engaging in poetic writing. Thus, any piece of writing will fall somewhere along Britton's continuum and it might reflect certain aspects of more than one type of written discourse. As Britton (1982) maintains, "We all use language in both these ways, to get things done in the outer world and to manipulate the inner world" (p. 36). The important things to remember are the writer's particular *purpose(s)* for writing and his intended *audience(s)*.

In this book I am concerned primarily with various kinds of expressive and poetic writing and reading. I have found over the years that these are the kinds of writing with which adult new readers and writers have had little experience. Often it was because during their school years they were in remedial or basic English classes where the emphasis was on worksheets, filling in the blanks, grammar exercises, and so on. Sometimes they simply felt that they were incompetent and unable to express themselves in writing or by creating a story or a poem. My hope is that the ideas, activities, and suggestions in this book will help adults who are less proficient than they want to be to see themselves in a new light, see themselves as writers. As the Canadian novelist Robertson Davies (1996) once observed, "A writer finds his themes and his characters in the depth of his own being, and his understanding of them is an understanding of himself" (p. 203). Expressive and poetic writing can help all of us, students and teachers alike, better understand ourselves and the world.

Modeling

We cannot help others become more literate and skilled in writing unless we as teachers also engage in the writing and reading that we ask them to do. I cannot stress strongly enough the importance of modeling for adults. It is vital that we show our students *how* we might go about writing a particular piece. Perhaps even more crucial is our demonstration of willingness to take the same kinds of risks with writing that we are asking them to take. I have found over the years that my students' success (at all ages) and my own have depended upon my active engagement with them as a fellow writer and reader, albeit one with more experience. This for me is the so-called bottom line of education as a democratic process. Therefore, all of the activities in this book are designed for both teachers and students working together as a community of writers and readers.

Classroom Structure

Based upon adults' "ways of knowing" research, Eleanor Drago-Severson (2004) has explored how they might best learn and the elements of a viable literacy program:

> Cohort relationships, collaborative learning, teacher-learner relationships, curricula, pedagogical practices, and program structure seemed to work synergistically to support and challenge these adult learners across a wide range of ways of knowing. (p. 153)

Accordingly, the activities in this book are based upon the importance of making writing an integral part of each class and not simply treating it as an afterthought. How we as adult educators arrange our classrooms is vitally important in the promotion of writing. Thus, I recommend the following arrangement (or one that reflects it in your own particular situation).

Desks are arranged in small circles facing each other to promote small-group and partner discussion. More student-led discussion and sharing is better than teacher-led discussion. As much as possible, students initiate writing based upon their own interests, needs, and goals. The lessons and ideas in this book should serve as catalysts for you and your students. As I will highlight throughout the lessons, whole-class, small-group, or partner discussions precede any writing. The point of such discussion is to elicit and share what each person knows and feels about a topic. This is especially important for your English-language learners (ELLs) who need opportunities to speak and listen to English in a supportive context.

Brainstorming, listing, note taking, or free writing of some sort usually follows discussion. It is here that modeling is important. Showing students examples of your rough notes and free writing with all of their scribbles, scrawls, abbreviations, cross outs, and misspellings will help them recognize that first attempts need not be perfect. Note taking is supported throughout by partner and group discussion. Then the particular form of writing is engaged with through organization and initial drafting. All three of these steps—discussion, note taking, and organization and drafting—in one way or another form the structure of most of the lessons.

An integral part of all of the lessons in this book is the opportunity for adults to voluntarily share something they have written at the beginning or conclusion of a class. I generally begin a class by asking if anyone has anything written that he wants to briefly share. This might be something the student has written since the last class meeting or something she has been working on for a while. Asking students to share with a partner or in small groups what they've been writing is also a good way to close a class. By providing opportunities for students to orally "publish" their writing with peers, they are able to experience pride in what they are creating. Most have had limited opportunities to do so during their educational experiences.

English-Language Learners

We will find in many, if perhaps not most, adult literacy classrooms a mixture of students, including those with varying degrees of proficiency in English. These adults might be highly literate in their home languages (and sometimes others), or they might have had only very limited schooling and literacy education in their countries of origin. Oftentimes an instructor or tutor with limited, if any, ELL training will find one or more such students in her class. How does she accommodate these students through the lessons and activities for the native English speakers?

This is not a book on ELL methodology for adult learners. There are fine resources available that focus specifically on literacy education for second-language learners, for example, *Talking Shop: A Curriculum Sourcebook for Participatory Adult ESL* (Nash et al., 1992), *Making Meaning, Making Change: Participatory Curriculum Development for Adult ESL Literacy* (Auerbach, 1992), and *Approaches to Adult ESL Literacy Instruction* (Crandall & Peyton, 1993). However, I do address the potential needs of ELLs throughout the book, realizing that some readers might have no background in working with these adults. My suggestions for modifications of lessons and alternative texts are meant to provide the reader with some general principles and strategies for teaching adult ELLs. I do so in each lesson by including a section titled "Keeping ELLs in Mind."

Underlying ELL Principles

Elsa Auerbach (1999) summarizes the consensus within the field of English for speakers of other languages concerning instructional principles and practices. Her points are important and provide the touchstones for all of my observations about adult ELL literacy instruction. Accordingly, I quote them at length. Auerbach (1999) observes,

> 1) that a focus on meaning rather than form (grammatical correctness) encourages writing development; 2) that instruction should stress writing for real reasons, to real audiences in order to promote authentic communication; 3) that writing should be contextualized and that content should be meaningful and relevant to learners; 4) that learners need some degree of overt instruction, which includes talk about writing, substantive, specific feedback, and multiple opportunities for revisions; 5) that social and cultural variation in writing practices and genres needs to be taken into account; and 6) that all writing pedagogy reflects a stance about the learner in relation to the social order. (pp. 4–5)

Correspondingly, the National Council of Teachers of English (2006) position paper on teaching ELLs in the mainstream classroom includes the following recommendations: providing authentic opportunities to use language in a nonthreatening environment; introducing cooperative, collaborative writing activities that promote discussion; providing frequent meaningful opportunities for students to generate their own texts; and choosing authentic materials that are written to inform or entertain, not to teach a grammar point or a letter–sound correspondence.

Stephen Krashen (1982) makes the distinction between language *acquisition* and language *learning*. *Language acquisition* is a "subconscious process; language acquirers are not usually aware of the fact that they are using language for communication." *Language learning*, on the other hand, refers to "conscious knowledge of a second language, knowing the rules, being aware of them, and being able to talk about them" (p. 10). The lessons in this book highlight language acquisition; however, exploration of rules, grammar, punctuation, and so forth—where appropriate—are also discussed.

These basic principles underpin four common assumptions of ELL literacy instruction:

1. Students' fluency with writing, reading, speaking, and listening precedes their ability to use language accurately. They must have a safe environment in which they can try out the second language in a variety of ways.

2. Accordingly, their acquisition of language function precedes the correct form, for example, "When I about 5 years old, I have learn my sewing" (Weinstein-Shr, 1994, p. 67).

3. Adults must be actively involved in using the language in real contexts for real purposes.

4. The literacy instructor and native English speakers in the class serve as language models and mentors.

Basic Strategies

The principles serve as guidelines for basic strategies that can be used in the adult literacy classroom.

1. Incorporate as much as possible students' particular strengths, for example, art, crafts, music, song (including those in the students' native language), and oral storytelling.

2. Model skilled reading from a wide range of texts during each class session, for example, prose fiction, poetry, myths and legends, magazines, newspapers, and so on.

3. Engage students during each class meeting in prepared oral reading as a social, collaborative activity, for example, choral readings, chants, songs, dramatic scripts, and so forth.

4. Highlight generative patterns of English that are regularly used. (See Graham, 1978, in several of the following lessons.)

5. Develop vocabulary in concrete situations, that is, help students actively use, manipulate, see, and hear words in different contexts, for example, in writing, role playing, photography, and exploration of environmental art.

6. Explicitly show students *how* to read, write, and use oral English by teaching specific strategies, for example, composing individual and collaborative Language Experience Approach (LEA) texts of different kinds (see Chapter 1 for more information about using LEA); modeling pre-, during-, and after-reading strategies; and encouraging active dialogue, reading, and writing between ELLs and native English speakers.

These basic strategies will be incorporated throughout the lessons in this book. With Elizabeth Chiseri-Strater (1994), I will emphasize the fact that literacy is fostered through "pedagogies that reinforce collaborative learning" such as "group work and peer tutoring…. Classrooms that emphasize group work and tutoring acknowledge cultural differences in the ways of displaying knowledge" (p. 183).

Overview

I have arranged the book into six chapters containing 23 specific lessons, all of which highlight different forms of expressive and/or poetic writing. Chapter 1 explores the uses of various kinds of journal writing. Chapter 2 highlights the writing of prose vignettes about one's world and oneself. Chapter 3 presents five lessons on different kinds of poetry writing easily accessible to those with even the most limited exposure to poetry. I include brief form poems such as the *lune* that I have found to be viable with less experienced writers. Chapter 4 makes the connection between writing and various kinds of music. Chapter 5 helps adults connect literacy with art through lessons that promote the use of classic paintings, everyday examples of artistic endeavors, and photography. Chapter 6 includes four lessons on the reading and writing of narrative and dramatic fictional texts.

Each chapter begins with an overview of the particular kind of writing that will be explored in the following lessons. The lessons themselves then follow a specific format: what to do in preparation for the lesson; how to engage adults in the lesson, often over more than one class meeting; what things to consider and adapt for the ELLs in your group; and finally how to extend the lesson in various ways.

Chapter 7 differs from the preceding six in form and content. In it I present *activities*, not complete lesson plans, that can be used as needed to help adults become more skillful in their writing with such things as revision, vocabulary use, spelling, punctuation, and grammar.

Throughout the lessons you will find examples of students' writing (all student names are pseudonyms) and my own. If you find them helpful, you may make copies for use with your students. Please note that all of the student examples have been edited for spelling and punctuation.

You also will find many examples from published writers. Please note the copyright notices in some of the credit lines before making copies for classroom use. Most publishers will grant permission for one-time educational use of a poem or excerpts from stories.

The lessons and activities presented in the seven chapters are based upon my experiences working with students in smaller and informal settings. When working with adults I seldom have more than 10 or so in a group. Accordingly, I do not suggest possible time frames for different parts of lessons. Depending upon your experience writing with adults, size and composition of the class, and the particular setting in which you teach, the amount of time for each lesson might range considerably from the same lesson taught by another person. The lessons are meant to be generative, that is, I want you to use them creatively and modify them as you see fit.

CHAPTER 1

Fostering Meaningful Writing With Journals

JOURNALS ARE THE touchstones of expressive writing. They allow us to record daily events that seem important. They help us capture our reactions to people and things and our particular moods at certain times. These are the things closest to ourselves and thus often a good place from which to begin writing with adults. Journal entries do not have to be long, be correct in terms of spelling, grammar, and punctuation, or be shared with others. They can be as private or public as the writers want them to be. The important thing is that they foster *daily* writing.

Students sometimes ask what they should put in their journals, and I usually respond by sharing a poem by the late William Stafford titled "What's in My Journal":

"What's in My Journal"

Odd things, like a button drawer. Mean
things, fishhooks, barbs in your hand.
But marbles too. A genius for being agreeable.
Junkyard crucifixes, voluptuous
discards. Space for knickknacks, and for
Alaska. Evidence to hang me, or to beatify.
Clues that lead nowhere, that never connected
anyway. Deliberate obfuscation, the kind
that takes genius. Chasms in character.
Loud omissions. Mornings that yawn above
a new grave. Pages you know exist
but you can't find them. Someone's terribly
inevitable life story, maybe mine.

(Stafford, 1998, p. 248) Copyright 1991, 1998
the estate of William Stafford. Reprinted from
The Way It Is: New & Selected Poems with the
permission of Graywolf Press, Saint Paul,
Minnesota, USA.

Stafford imparts the notion that a journal is a place for anything and everything. It allows us to note the commonplace, the trivial, and those things of importance. However, a journal also is a place for reflecting on ourselves and sometimes for being brutally honest. Ultimately, Stafford says, this hodgepodge might even tell us who we are.

A journal can serve as a writing cache, that is, a place for storing ideas, images, insights, words, and bits of conversation that we might not share with others. A few entries from the diary shared with me by a man in one of my writing groups illustrate the brief, commonplace observations that a journal might contain. His grandmother kept this diary in rural Minnesota, USA.

November 15, 1899
Theo will finish breaking timothy today.
It is a beautiful weather for this time of year.

November 29, 1899
Theo grubbing stumps.
Rainy and spitting snow.

November 20, 1913
The men are husking corn.
Ground thawing out.
Theo plowing corn stubble ground.
We are shredding corn this afternoon.

Notice that even in these seemingly commonplace observations interesting images—bits of poetry—jump out: "breaking timothy," "grubbing stumps," and "spitting snow."

The three lessons included in this chapter highlight the use of journals as an easy and vital way of fostering meaningful writing among adult basic literacy students. Although related and overlapping in various ways, each lesson focuses on a particular kind of journal writing: daily observation, overheard conversation, and personal reflection. The lessons are designed to give you structure, but you should not be afraid to modify and perhaps extend them as you begin writing with your students.

Daily Observation Journals

In order to develop their literacy abilities, adults must read and write on a regular, if not daily, basis. Literacy is a practice, and like all practices, whether knitting, fly fishing, or bread baking, the more we engage in it for real purposes the more skilled we'll likely become. Unfortunately, sometimes adults see writing as something that they do in class but not outside of it. This lesson highlights writing as an everyday endeavor by encouraging students to observe and record in brief sentences, phrases, and words the world around them. It promotes writing as a *habit* that leads to writing of different kinds, for example, stories, poems, dramatic scripts, letters, e-mails, and so on.

BEFORE THE LESSON

1 Read through the complete lesson and estimate how long it might take with your particular group of students. Decide if any of your ELLs will need additional assistance.

2 Share a poem such as William Stafford's "What's in My Journal." Practice reading it aloud several times. If you think Stafford's poem might be too difficult for your students, especially for your ELLs, because of some of the vocabulary, unrhymed lines, and poetic leaps and connections, I've included a poem that I wrote (obviously not of the same quality!) that attempts to capture the same general idea but which might be easier to understand. (Better yet, write one of your own!)

> "Things in My Journal"
>
> My father's watch that doesn't run.
> A dead carp left rotting in the sun.
> The little red wagon I pulled as a child.
> Times when I'm angry and when I'm mild.
> The golden earring of an old lover,
> And the pain when she left me for another.
> Memories that don't add up to a lot.
> Things that I've lost and those I've still got
> Like pocketknives, shells, pieces of drivel,
> Voices, songs, and snatches of riddles.
> I'm not sure whose journal this might be,
> At times when I read it I think that it's me.

3 Be prepared to share examples from your own daily journal. You might print these on an overhead transparency, on a flip chart, on the dry-erase board, or you might make copies for your students.

4 Obtain a new journal notebook for each student. I have found that the 3 × 5 inch memo book works best, but you might also consider something slightly larger. You want students to be able to carry the notebook in a shirt or pants pocket or in a purse. (You can buy these inexpensively at office supply stores or at major retailers.)

THE LESSON, PART I

1 Ask if anyone has ever kept a journal or a diary; if anyone has, ask him or her to share when and how it was kept. Briefly explain to the students your plans for the lesson.

2 Use Stafford's poem (or my alternative version) and ask the students to follow along as you read it. Read it a second time, and be sure to capture the rhythm of the poem. Then ask the students to read along with you a third time. Rereading, especially of poetry, is vitally important for all readers, adults as well as children.

3 Ask students what they think about the poem. (Don't ask what it "means" because that implies there is a single, "correct" meaning to a poem.) You might have to clarify certain words for all students, for example, *obfuscation* and *chasms*; and particular cultural references for ELLs, for example, *button drawer* and *knickknacks*. (My poem should present little difficulty.) Give students plenty of time to reflect and respond. Have partners or trios first share among themselves before they share with the whole class. Sharing among themselves is a safe way of encouraging a variety of insights. You want, as much as possible, for all students to respond, but be prepared for initial reticence or silence. Remember that many adult basic literacy students have learned over the years to be silent in class and to expect that the teacher has all of the "correct" answers.

4 After everyone has had a chance to respond to the poem and you have clarified any new vocabulary, read the poem again as a whole group.

5 Point out that one of the things that's interesting about the poem is the way Stafford says he puts anything in his journal—commonplace everyday things that he sees about him—for example, a button drawer, fishhooks, marbles, crucifixes, discards, knickknacks, pages, and so forth. Also note that he includes more abstract things, for example, chasms in character. (I try to do the same thing in mine, for example, my father's watch, dead carp, earring, pain, memories, snatches of drivel, and so on.)

6 Show your own daily journal and describe how you use it to jot down interesting, unusual, or new things that you encounter every day. Highlight how you also include strange or unique words that you find on billboards and street signs. Display a number of entries from your journal as examples. Here are some from mine:

2/5/05
red oak leaves
pines creaking in wind
blue juniper berries
melting snow

7/11/05
Myrt's restaurant
home fried potatoes
Voyageur Days
loggers
roughnecks

7/30/05
Pentagoet Inn
Castine Maine
Dennett's Wharf
Farnsworth Museum
Black Bull
Haskell Island
Rockland

Lime Rock Inn
Sequin Room

9/2/05
12 perch
bluegills
coyote
slag heap
rust ruins
crow calling

7 Share with students the value of keeping a daily journal. It helps you remember particular times and places; serves as a place for storing words and phrases that you might use in future writing; and most important, it encourages you to write *something*, however brief, every day. Pass your journal around so that students can see that such things as neat handwriting, complete sentences, and correct spelling are not important in a daily journal.

8 Distribute the little journals to the students. Tell them that as part of the class you're encouraging them to keep one on a regular, if not daily, basis. Depending upon your particular location, have students walk about for 10 minutes looking closely at what's around them and jotting down in their journals whatever they see that is interesting to them. (It's best to go outside, but if that's not possible the students can walk around inside the building or even simply look around the classroom or in their own pockets and purses.) Be sure to participate along with your students, jotting down in your journal what you see.

9 Encourage your native English speakers to spell the best they can as they write, and tell them that later, if they desire, you will help them with correct spellings. (Spelling shouldn't count in a daily journal, but I've found that too many adult literacy students are unduly concerned with correctness as a result of prior schooling. As often as possible, assure students that spelling will be addressed later.)

10 If you have ELLs in your class whose English is very limited, and if they are literate in their native language, ask them to either make their journal entries as best as they can in English or to make them in their home language. Explain to them that you'll later work with them in terms of spelling.

11 After 10 minutes gather back as a class and ask for volunteers to share what they wrote in their journals. (You share too!) Make a list on chart paper or the dry-erase board. Ask how many people noticed something that they didn't pay any attention to before. Be sure to impress upon them that this process is what good writers employ; they look closely at the world around them and make a record of what they see. Good writing emphasizes particulars and not abstractions.

12 Ask your students to keep a daily journal for a week. Ask them to try to write something every day. Once again, tell them what they write doesn't have to be long and doesn't have to be spelled correctly. Encourage them to notice the things around them in their homes, neighborhood, and on the job. If they see some interesting signs, billboards, or advertisements on television that catch their attention, tell them to jot those down too.

13 Instruct the students to bring their journals to class the following week. (If you meet with your students daily or more than once a week, give them a full week in which to begin their journals; that way you'll be more likely to have enough entries with which to work as a class.)

THE LESSON, PART 2

1 In order to get back into the spirit of journal keeping, read Stafford's poem (or mine, or better yet, yours), and then reread it as a whole class.

2 Debrief with the students about their journal writing during the past week. What did they find interesting? Where were they best able to write in their journals? When? What problems might have occurred or what might have hindered their writing?

3 Have partners share one or more of their entries. Then ask for volunteers to share with the whole class. Write the entries on chart paper or the dry-erase board. (Use correct spelling.) Here are a couple of examples from students:

>recipes for fish
>chicken broth
>cook
>chef school
>chef certificate
>good food
>fast food
>beef patties
>
>leather wallet
>driver's license
>fishing license
>hunting license
>pictures of my kids
>Glenda
>Frank
>Cheryl
>mad money just in case

4 Highlight the diversity of the journal entries. Journals allow students to focus on those things that are of interest to them. Pay special attention to the specifics that students have written. Once again, stress the importance of concrete particulars in writing.

5 Ask students to select one entry or words from several entries that they'd like to use as a catalyst for a brief piece of writing. Give them a few minutes to discuss possible choices with a partner.

6 Once they have selected an entry or entries have them discuss with their partners what they might write. Emphasize that the piece of writing does not need to be longer than a sentence or two. Circulate among the students and assist where needed.

7 Allow 10 minutes for writing on loose-leaf sheets of paper. If necessary, help your ELLs, especially those with very limited English ability. You might use a Language Experience Approach (LEA) and assist them with the actual writing. If you are unfamiliar with LEA methodology, it is simply the transcription of what a student dictates to you. The value of LEA is that it allows students to see their oral language captured in print, and it allows them to focus on meaningful content instead of trying to get the spelling and punctuation correct. It's important for students to actually see you writing their words. I typically say each word as I'm writing it and then repeat each sentence. Rereading and repetition are important. If I'm going to use LEA with a student or a group of students, I always say, "Well, now, you dictate and I'll be your secretary." Have partners share their first drafts, and then ask for volunteers to share. Here's a final, reworked draft of the leather wallet journal entry by Tim:

> I keep everything I need in my wallet. I keep my driver's license, fishing and hunting licenses, kids' pictures and extra money just in case. My daughter Cheryl gave it to me for my birthday. I keep my old one in the bedroom drawer.

8 After volunteers have shared, have students put their first drafts in their working writing folders. If you have immediate access to a copy machine, you can make copies (with students' permission) and later explore what common needs there might be among students in terms of writing mechanics and spelling. You can then base future skills lessons on these needs. (We'll further explore such skills as spelling, punctuation, and grammar in Chapter 7.)

KEEPING ELLs IN MIND

1 ELLs might be silent during whole-group discussion and sharing. That's not unusual. They also might appear to be passive, but they're not. They are simply tuning in to the words and rhythms of what's being said, and trying to understand what's going on in the particular context. That's why some scholars maintain that at the beginning, second-language instruction should emphasize listening (Asher, 1977). Partner or small-group discussion and sharing with native English speakers provides ELLs with a safer context in which to try out the new language.

2 If you have ELLs who are not literate in their home language and know very little English, encourage them to write down something, even initial letters or sounds, during the 10-minute walk-around and journal writing at the start of the lesson. For example, I've had *t* for *tree*, *sh* for *squirrel*, and so on. If even that is not possible, then you can walk around with them and jot down words and phrases in their little journals as they point out things to you. If you have any native English speakers in the class who are competent with basic writing, they also can serve as scribes for individual ELLs.

3 Have ELLs use their journals as English word caches. During the week they can note new, confusing, or interesting words they encounter at work, in the supermarket, in their children's textbooks, and so on. When they bring these words back to the classroom, you can use them to help the students compose short texts in an LEA manner. Later these little texts can serve as a basis for teaching various skills (as we'll explore in Chapter 7).

WRAP UP

1 Encourage students to continue writing in their journals. Explain that you will begin each class with the sharing of journal entries. (And, of course, you will share your journal and the more extended writing that you do based on particular entries.) Use these journal entries as an integral part of your class writing activities.

2 As you encourage daily observation writing and expand into other types of journal keeping, you will be demonstrating to your students that writing allows them to capture and hold bits and pieces of their lives in the daily flow of things. Moreover, you will be showing them that writing need not be long or difficult. By fostering partner and group sharing of journals and drafts you will not only help students look closely at how written language works but also will help them see the power of literacy as a personal and social process.

Overheard Conversation Journals

This lesson promotes writing grounded in the language of different people that we encounter in our own communities. It acknowledges and values the living speech of individuals no matter who they are; the crusty humor of the construction laborer, current slang of the hip hop teenager, and old-fashioned phrases of the 99-year-old woman are as linguistically rich (and often more so) as the college-educated professional. James Paul Gee (2008) observes that "both standard and non-standard dialects are marvels of human mastery. Neither is better or worse" (p. 21). Listening more closely to and then writing about other people's language will help adults develop a better appreciation for language diversity and a facility for incorporating dialogue into their writing.

BEFORE THE LESSON

1 Carl Sandburg (1958), the Chicago poet, once observed that people often talk poetry without knowing it. He said that if we listen closely to what people say we will hear interesting expressions and phrases, funny stories and anecdotes, and a wealth of words including dialect and slang that we will be able to use in our own writing.

Conversation journals, or what I sometimes call "eavesdropping" or "spy" journals, help us begin to notice the rich language around us and then capture it in writing. We are now engaging in what James Britton (1982) calls "poetic" writing, that is, with conscious word choice and the construction of something special with language. We take on the role of a "spectator." This allows us to step back and look at other people's language as we create something unique, some little work of art. As Britton observes,

> I've suggested that in the spectator role we show a concern for the total world picture, a concern for the total context into which every experience has to be fitted. I've suggested that creating a world is to some extent a social process. (p. 105)

2 Begin to capture in your own journal bits and pieces of conversations that you hear every day. Try to include both those that you've overheard and those in which you've taken part. Keep your journal for at least two weeks so that you'll have a variety of examples to share with your students. Here are some examples from my own journal:

Overheard:

[While walking down the street] "And he was just sitting there, picking fluff, of all things, from his bellybutton!"

[Three men in khaki work clothes eating steaks in a restaurant] "Yeah, Julia Child's veal recipes are superior."

[At an American Legion Post bar] "Hi, Margie, how's it goin' kid?"
"I'm here, ain't I? That's somethin'."

In Conversation:

[At a farm] "I've been out pickin' peas. My daughter's comin' home and we're gonna have a pea fest!"

[At a Bed & Breakfast in Scotland] "I'm retired but I still work as a lollipop man [a school crossing guard who holds up a sign or "lollipop"]."

[A cowboy at a dude ranch] "I herd cattle or people. It's all the same. It's all herding."

3 Locate or prepare conversation poems such as those by William Carlos Williams:

"Detail"

Hey!
Can I have some more
milk?

YEEEEAAAAASSSSS!
—always the gentle
mother!

(Williams, 1988b, p. 19) By William Carlos Williams,
from *Collected Poems 1939–1962, Volume II*, copyright
1944 by William Carlos Williams. Reprinted by permission
of New Directions Publishing Corp.

"Detail"

Doc, I bin lookin' for you
I owe you two bucks.

How you doin'?

Fine. When I get it
I'll bring it up to you.

(Williams, 1988a, pp. 20–21) By William Carlos
Williams, from *Collected Poems 1939–1962,
Volume II,* copyright 1944 by William Carlos
Williams. Reprinted by permission of New
Directions Publishing Corp.

4   Practice reading aloud the poems in a vigorous conversational manner, highlighting the poet's use of vernacular speech, that is, "I bin lookin' for you," and "How you doin'?"

THE LESSON, PART I

1   Ask the students how often they have overheard snatches of talk or the conversations of strangers that were interesting, humorous, or intriguing. If one or two people want to share, have them do so. Ask them if they remember where and when they heard the conversations. Then briefly share your plans for the lesson.

2   Share the poems by Williams by asking the students to follow along as you read them. Read with much dramatic vigor, and read each one at least twice. Have the students as a whole group read the poems with you.

3   Tell the students that these are examples of conversational poems in which one or two people are talking. Have partners read the two poems in which two people are talking. Ask them to read the poems twice, taking turns with the different speakers in the poems. ELLs can readily participate with lines as simple as "How you doin'?"

4   Ask for volunteers to read to the whole class. Point out that the poems capture everyday spoken language and that Williams uses phonetic spelling to convey such language in print, for example, "bin lookin'."

5   Share the examples from your journal. You might make copies of these for the students or simply write them on chart paper or the dry-erase board. Explain where, when, and how you got these bits of talk. Tell them that their little journals are ideal for jotting down conversations, phrases, and words that they overhear in a supermarket or restaurant, on the job, or in a bus. Tell them that they are also good for noting conversations in which they participate. Stress that writers of all kinds, not only poets but also novelists, dramatists, and journalists, do this kind of listening and note taking. In addition to being fun to keep, such journal entries will help them expand their writing caches and provide possible sources for future writing.

6 Instruct your students to begin adding conversations and snatches of talk to their daily observation journals. Tell them that the more they listen the more they will hear. Share your strategy of jotting down immediately or shortly after hearing it any brief conversation, phrase, expression, or word that you find interesting, funny, or unusual.

7 Encourage your students to try to capture at least 10 but hopefully more pieces of talk in their journals during the next two weeks. (This time frame will vary according to your students, the structure of your class sessions, and how often you meet. You can foster such entries by sharing and having one or two volunteers share each time you gather as a class.) Tell them that they don't have to write *exactly* what they heard because that's often very difficult to do. They simply should try to write the overheard talk as best as they can.

THE LESSON, PART 2

1 Begin the lesson by sharing some entries from your own journal. Highlight one or more in which you were an eavesdropper and at least one in which you were a participant. Ask partners to share one or two of their favorites. Then have volunteers share with the whole class.

2 At this point you have options. The students might follow the same process from the daily observation writing and transcribe one or more journal entries in first and subsequent drafts. For example, here's Mike's:

> "I quit!" he said.
> "Why?"
> "I didn't like working as a painter. I told the boss it was a messy job."

3 You might also help the students shape an entry into a poem in the manner of Williams. Use one of your own entries as a model. Here's what I did with the "pea fest" entry:

> The boy tells us
> He'll go get Stub.
> Five minutes later
> Stubby drives from behind
> the barn on a 4-wheeler,
> boy holding on the back.
> A grizzled character,
> he might be a hippie
> settler from the 60s who stayed
> and appears not to have bathed since.
> "I've been out pickin' peas—
> my daughter's comin' home
> and we're gonna have a pea fest!"

4 If students want to shape one or more entries into a poem, stress that the poems don't have to rhyme (but they might) or be of any particular length. (We'll address different kinds of poetry writing in Chapter 3.) As an initial attempt you might want to ask for one of the students' entries and shape it as a class into a poem. Model how when creating a poem you will almost certainly add (sometimes much) to the journal entry. Here's Dave's journal entry followed by the class reshaping:

"You won't last three weeks."
"I'll bet you three years."

You won't last three weeks.
I'll bet you three years.
I took the bet.
That was fifteen years ago.
I guess I won.

5 The poem can also be shaped into a dialogue poem for two voices. (We'll also explore different kinds of dramatic scripts in Chapter 6.) Conversation journal entries are especially viable for such poetry and the subsequent choral reading. Here's how the class reshaped the poem into one for two voices:

"You Won't Last"

(Voice 2)	(Voice 1)
I'll bet you	
three weeks.	three years.
I took the bet.	
Fifteen years ago	Fifteen years ago.
	I guess I won.

6 Encourage students as a whole class, in small groups, with partners, or as individuals to experiment with different ways of working with their conversation journal entries.

KEEPING ELLs IN MIND

1 This is an appropriate place for ELLs to interact meaningfully with their native English-speaking peers. Together they can create texts that will be read as oral performances. ELLs will have opportunities to explore, hear, and try out vernacular English in a safe and supportive setting (Rigg & Kazemek, 1993).

2 We'll explore Carolyn Graham's jazz chants (1978) for ELLs in Chapter 6. They also emphasize vernacular English, and some of them offer alternative ways of saying the same thing, for example, the polite "Please be quiet" and the rude "Shut up." Conversation journals are great places for capturing and contrasting spoken forms of English.

3 Again, ELLs can use their journals as English word caches. They can note new, confusing, or interesting words and expressions they hear at work, in the supermarket, and out in the community (for example, "It cracks me up," and "He kicked the bucket"). When they bring these words and expressions back to the classroom, you can use them to help the students compose short texts in an LEA format. Later these little texts can serve as a basis for teaching various skills.

WRAP UP

Encourage students to write in their journals, including the interesting, unusual, or new objects, words, and things they encounter each day and the bits and pieces of conversation they hear or in which they participate. Continue to use these journal entries as an integral part of your class and as opportunities for fostering different kinds of reading and writing.

Personal Reflection Journals

As I've noted in the Introduction, print literacy is both social and personal. There are many different *literacies* in which people engage for any number of reasons. This lesson fosters writing as a particularly personal process. The journals that you encourage adults to keep are for their eyes only. Indeed, this lesson builds on what even less skilled literacy students are sometimes already doing in terms of keeping a diary.

BEFORE THE LESSON

1 Personal journals are perhaps the best examples of what James Britton (1982) calls "expressive" writing. They allow us to reflect on our daily lives, deepest feelings, fears, joys, loves, and hates. As I am using the term here, a personal reflection journal is synonymous with "diary." In her detailed study of ordinary Americans born between 1895 and 1985 Deborah Brandt (2001) found that "[m]any people I interviewed reported using private writing to purge feelings, primarily anger or grief. Much of this writing was never shown to anyone and was, in fact, destroyed" (p. 162). Therefore, lessons built around personal journals should only serve to promote individual writing as a safe "space" for exploring private emotions and perhaps venting one's frustrations, anger, and so forth. Personal journal entries are not appropriate for public reading or sharing.

2 Locate a short selection to share with students such as the following one from R.S. Thomas's yearlong journal titled "A Year in Llyn" (1997). Thomas was an Anglican priest whom many believe to have been the greatest Welsh poet of the 20th century.

> March—the month of my birth! It is without doubt an exciting month, one that sees the earth waking from its deep sleep. It is also a turbulent month, one that brings the turn

of the wheel toward us, with its strong winds and the first migrants amongst the birds. Am I glad to have been born? There's a question! Yeats said that he would be willing to live it all again. Would I? An answer to the contrary seems abhorrent. Compared with so many wretches who are blind and lame or sick, I have so much to be grateful for. (pp. 124–125)

3 Keep a personal journal for several weeks. Select one or more entries that you think would serve as models and that you would be willing to share with your students. Make copies for them. Here are a couple of examples from my journal:

[In Amsterdam airport] Lack of excitement—stomach flutters of youth are gone—jaded? tired? living in small towns too long? Tired—sleepy—can't think of anything profound.

[At outdoor café on coast of Maine] Fat man with strong southern drawl—wife tagging behind—T-shirt with confederate flag on the back—picture of Robert E. Lee on the front with "Officer and Gentleman"—insensitive jerk—lucky he's not in a more diverse setting.

THE LESSON

1 Review with your students the kinds of journal writing that they have been doing, that is, daily observations and capturing conversations. Ask if anyone also has been using his journal to write private feelings or things that he would not want others to see, for example, anger at or disappointment over a friend's comments. Tell your students that journals are perfect places for such personal reflections. We can be brutally honest with ourselves, and we can record observations about others that we would never think of sharing with them. The audience for personal reflection journals is ourselves.

2 Share R.S. Thomas's journal entry by having students follow along as you read it aloud. Read it a second time. You might want to point out that Thomas was an elderly man when he wrote this and that he was both an Anglican priest and a poet. Tell them that "Yeats" was W.B. Yeats the great Irish poet. Llyn is an isolated area on the northern coast of Wales. If you have access to a map of the British Isles, you might want to point out the coast of Wales.

3 Ask the students what they think about the entry. Have they ever asked the same sort of question as Thomas? Have them share their thoughts with a partner or perhaps in trios. Then open up the discussion for the whole class.

4 Hand out copies of entries from your own personal journal. Highlight how you use it to express your feelings at different times. Explain to students that your personal journal often allows you deal with sadness (for example, my first entry) or such strong emotions as disgust (for example, my second entry).

5 Tell students that in addition to giving them a safe place to reflect on their lives and feelings at particular times, personal journals will help them get in the habit of writing regularly. Share with them your own habits. Perhaps you write in your journal early in the morning or at the end of the day. Perhaps on some days you write a lot, and on other days little or nothing at all. You don't worry about spelling, grammar, or punctuation. You simply write about your thoughts and feelings.

6 Emphasize that these private journals are also caches that they might use for other kinds of writing. Because they typically contain strong emotions, some entries might be developed into such things as love poems. A student named Ron used several of his private journal reflections about his wife as the basis for a poem that concluded, "I'm happy she is my wife./She's all of my life./My wife is a blessing to me."

7 Encourage students to expand their journal writing to include such personal or diary-like entries. They might want to use a separate notebook for this purpose. Urge them to find a daily time and place to write their reflections. Inform them that these journals will not be shared in class.

KEEPING ELLs IN MIND

If your ELLs are literate in their home language you might suggest that they keep their personal reflection journals in that language. They most likely will be able to express their deepest thoughts and feelings better in their native language than in English. Moreover, you will be recognizing and honoring literacy in multiple languages.

WRAP UP

1 On a regular basis, perhaps weekly, ask your students how many have written in their personal journals. Share the number of times that you have done so. Don't ask for anyone to share; however, I have found that sometimes individuals do want to share what they've written and how they feel. Give them the opportunity. It can be necessary and important for them to do so.

2 In this lesson on personal reflection journals I have emphasized a particular focus just as I have done with the lessons on daily observation and conversation journals. Obviously, all three kinds of journal writing overlap. I have elaborated each one in order to demonstrate the possibilities for engaging adults in brief, daily, and personal writing. The lessons are meant as possible guides or structures to use as is or to modify or combine as you see fit. Your particular group of students, classroom arrangement, and regularity of meeting times will all have a direct effect on how you incorporate journals and your literacy curriculum. It is vitally important, I believe, that you do so in some meaningful manner.

Moving From Storytelling to Writing Prose Vignettes

A
S HUMANS WE TELL countless stories every day; indeed, we are the storytelling animal. We take this unique ability for granted, seldom giving it any consideration:

"What did you do last night?"
"Not much. Watched a little TV."
"Yeah, so did I, *Law and Order*."
"I watched that, too. Wasn't it scary? It reminded me of that incident in town last summer."
"I think it was based on that. Whatever happened to that guy?"

"Gosh, look at that photograph of when we were young."
"You had more hair, and I had fewer wrinkles, that's for sure."
"That was one of our best trips."
"Remember what happened right after that guy took our picture?"
"Oh, man, do I! The ferry lost power in the middle of Puget Sound and...."

Such daily storytelling is as natural to us as breathing. The novelist and essayist Dennis Covington (1994) captures the wonder of storytelling as an almost miraculous human power: "At the heart of the impulse to tell stories is a mystery so profound that even as I begin to speak of it, the hairs on the back of my hand are starting to stand on end" (p. 691).

Stories and storytelling are what all adults bring to a literacy class. It is their strength: the ability to talk of their own lives and to listen to others share their particular life experiences. As Roger Schank (1990) observes, "Conversation is no more than responsive storytelling" (p. 24). Writing prose vignettes as an integral part of the adult literacy class helps students play their strong suit. Prose vignettes of *any* length foster the transformation of oral speech into written language. For example, many years ago I taught a class with my wife (a mental health social worker) for people with various mental illnesses. One man in the class was the closest I have ever encountered to being truly "illiterate." At the beginning he had a hard time recognizing his name in print. His first piece of writing came from shared stories of Christmases in our pasts:

"Christmas as a Kid"

We always had a tree with lights.
Mom and Dad always bought presents.
My favorite was a BB gun.

What is a prose vignette? It is simply a brief description or a short sketch or story. Think of an incident or a scene in a movie. Think of "Christmas as a Kid." A vignette might tell of a particular life experience or it might simply describe something we see, hear, smell, touch, or taste. Here's a work vignette by Jerry:

I was offered a job as foreman, but I had to turn the job down because I could not read or spell well.
But I like the job I have done for 30-some years as a crane operator.

And here is a description vignette by Douglas titled "Fall":

We cover the flowerbeds to keep off the frost and save the beauty of the different colors. We try to keep the beauty of nature as long as possible.
Trees start to change their leaves from green to many colors before they all fall to the ground. We drive around to see all of the dying beauty and remember.

Prose vignettes can be about almost anything, and that's their value in the literacy classroom. Their roots in our natural abilities as storytellers make them indispensable.

Robert McAfee Brown (1988) says that writing is "a kind of magic" (pp. 333–334), and reading is, too. We write for many reasons, he continues, but often we write because we want to change things. From my own experience with writers of all abilities and ages I believe the things we want to change most are our images of ourselves, our views of the world, and, indeed, our life stories. A friend reminds me that there is always the possibility of "re-storying" our lives. Indeed, many writers say that they write in order to process their own lives. When we write, Brown maintains, we live within a "community of writers" (pp. 333–334). The possibility of change and the magic of writing occur as we talk, explore, storytell, and put pen to paper or fingers to a keyboard within a supportive context of other writers. The lessons in this chapter highlight the importance of engaging two dimensions of James Britton's (1982) "universe of discourse," that is, expressive and poetic writing, through the creation of prose vignettes. The lessons are representative and should serve as springboards to many other writing activities. I pay special attention to vignettes that help us look at the world with fresh eyes and recognize the value in our everyday vernacular language.

What might our students and we write about? Anything. Everything. Following are some general topics that I have found to be generative. However, once you begin to brainstorm possible writing ideas with your students, you will find that the list is seemingly endless. Some topics with which to begin include the following:

- Stories of work, both good and bad jobs
- Stories of different "firsts," for example, first day at school, first love, and so on
- Stories about family members, friends, and special people that you've known
- Stories about memorable places
- Stories you remember others telling you in the past
- Stories of "adventures" that you had in your life
- Descriptions of both everyday and special objects, places, animals, and so on
- Reflections on spiritual, meditative, or religious matters

In this chapter we will explore four particular prose vignette lessons: vignettes about work, vignettes about people and things, vignettes about things of the spirit, and oral history vignettes about other people. I also will suggest other possible topics in the following chapters.

Vignettes About Work

This lesson highlights expressive writing, that is, writing that is closest to ourselves. It explores how we feel and think about a particular job or jobs that we had in the past or that we have at present. It allows us to reflect fondly or to vent frustration and anger. We might laugh at ourselves or others. Prose vignettes about work almost always evoke strong feelings and memories and result in meaningful writing.

BEFORE THE LESSON

1   Read through the complete lesson and estimate how long it might take with your particular group of students. Determine if any of your ELLs will need additional assistance. I have found that with a small group of students, say, 10 to 15, the first part of this lesson will take between 30 to 45 minutes. However, it is important to keep in mind that the time will vary according to the composition of your students, the particular situation, and your own experience as a writer. For example, I never work with large groups of students: 10 to 12 tends to be the average number. Thus, if you are working with larger groups, you'll have to take that into consideration as you are planning the lesson.

2   Locate a prose vignette that focuses on work to share with students such as the following selection from Studs Terkel's collection of oral histories, *American Dreams: Lost & Found* (1980). A former insurance salesman and now New York City cab driver, Ben Green, reflects on his job.

So I went to the cab in '69. Now I drive regular.

At the beginning it killed me. I picked up a man one day, a professional cello player. He gets in with a Hungarian accent and says: "You're not a cab driver." I said: "What makes you think so?" The first words he says: "I know, I can look at you." I felt good.

I had a low feeling about cab drivers. I still do. I don't like to mention it, I put it in the closet. I tell people: "Don't tell 'em I'm a cab driver." I could hold my own with most people....

I'm makin' a livin'. I'm probably makin' more now than I'd be makin' in insurance. But it's that image again. Why am I so concerned with image? Guys peddle, guys shovel horse shit. Why am I so concerned with my image? (pp. 220–221)

3 Write your own work vignette and make copies for your students. Here's mine as an example.

"Working the Night Shift"

I'd shuffle in with the others in a long, ragged column to the time clock. We'd punch in with two minutes to spare.

Usually I'd work with Betty and Slim, putting silver washers and nuts on auto gauges for ten hours with overtime.

In the din of the beveling presses pounding out the gauges I'd dream of a life somewhere out West, maybe the New Mexican desert with its turquoise sky and smell of pines.

THE LESSON, PART I

1 Briefly explain your plans for the lesson.

2 Ask your students if they've had a job or jobs that they've really liked. What about one that they've disliked? How do they feel about their present job, whether outside or in the home? Ask volunteers to share. Discuss briefly what might make a good job or a bad job.

3 Share the brief selection from Terkel's (1980) book by having students follow along as you read the selection out loud. As a whole class, read it a second time. Depending upon your particular group of students, ask if anyone wants to read it a third time. (As I'll continue to stress, rereading is important, both for native English speakers and, especially, for your ELLs.)

4 Ask your students what they think of the piece. Encourage an open discussion. Some prompts that you might keep in mind—only if needed—include the following:

• Do you think Ben Green likes his job? Why or why not?

• Why is he so defensive about his image as a cab driver?

- Why did he feel good when the cello player told him he wasn't really a cab driver?
- What value does the larger society and popular media place on different occupations, say, service jobs compared with professional ones? Why?
- What does Ben think about such valuing [Guys peddle, guys shovel horse shit]?
- How do they [your students] feel about such distinctions?

5 Point out, in case no one has commented, that Terkel uses *'em*, *livin'*, and *makin'* in order to capture vernacular language or the way people talk. (Refer back to the lesson Conversation Journals in Chapter 1.)

6 Distribute copies of your work vignette. Read it aloud a couple of times. Answer any questions the students might have about your prose vignette, for example, when and where you had the job, and so forth.

7 Compare your feelings about the job in your work vignette with those of Ben Green. I, for example, disliked the tedium of my factory job, and the pay wasn't very good. Ben appears ambivalent—concerned with his image but satisfied with the money he is making.

8 Tell your students that both pieces of writing are work vignettes. A vignette is a little sketch, story, or description. Tell them a vignette can be about almost anything and it can be of any length.

9 Ask partners to share with each other jobs that they liked or disliked. Allow a few minutes for the sharing.

10 Ask for volunteers and list on the dry-erase board or chart paper the various jobs and the reasons for liking or disliking them. (You might make columns for "Jobs Liked," "Why," "Jobs Disliked," "Why.") This whole-class discussion usually helps individuals focus on jobs they want to describe in writing.

11 Ask individuals to begin writing their work vignettes. (At this point in the process don't worry about spelling, grammar, and so forth. However, as I have already discussed in Chapter 1, I have found that some adults, due to their past school experiences, fixate on correct spelling and stop writing if they don't know how to spell a word. Circulate among the students with a pad of sticky notes, and if you see this happening simply write the word spelled correctly—that is, if you know how!—and give it to the individual. We'll further explore spelling in Chapter 7.)

12 Assist ELLs with their writing when needed. This might require an LEA approach where you or perhaps another more skilled student take dictation from the less skilled adult.

13 Ask for volunteers to share their first drafts. Introduce the notion of "appreciations," that is, telling the writer one specific thing you liked about the vignette. For example, here is Dan's first draft:

> I worked at Kowalski's for 3 years, 2 weeks and three days. I was a dishwasher. I took too many smoke breaks and got fired.
>
> I moved on to F.R.B. Dining as a dishwasher. I got fired for fighting with another worker. I was there for 3 months, 2 weeks, and 4 days.
>
> I hate dishwashing.

I told Dan I liked his strong ending and the way it naturally followed from the two preceding paragraphs. Another student appreciated how Dan captured the tedious nature of dishwashing by listing the years, weeks, and days.

14 Review with your students what they've done in the lesson: explored what we mean by a prose vignette; thought and talked about one or more jobs they've had; written a first draft of their work vignettes; and listened to others read, paying special attention to particular things in the writing that they appreciated or liked.

15 Have the students put away their first drafts until the next class meeting.

THE LESSON, PART 2

1 Ask the students to take out the first drafts of their work vignettes and reread them. Then have partners share. Stress the value of putting away a piece of writing for a while (days or longer), letting it "incubate," and then coming back to it with fresh eyes. Tell them this is what most professional writers do. They revise or re-vision (see again) what they have written.

2 Introduce the structure that newspaper writers use, that is, the reporter's 5Ws & H: Who, What, Where, When, Why, and How. Tell students that this is a viable way of organizing their ideas and writing, especially with prose vignettes. Use your own vignette as an example of how this might work and then use one from a volunteer. As examples, consider the following:

Who: I (Francis)

What: Assembly line work

Where: A gauge factory

When: The night shift

Why: Make money

How: Didn't like it: "shuffle in," dreaming of the West

Who: Dan

What: Washing dishes

Where: Kowalski's and F.R.B. Dining

When: 3 years, and so forth

Why: Make money

How: Hated it

3   Ask students to look at their own vignettes and see if they might add anything using the 5Ws & H as a guide in order to make them more descriptive or complete. (Stress that the 5Ws & H are simply *guides*; often times something can be put in one or more of the categories. For example, my *What* could be *assembly line work in a gauge factory*.) Circulate and assist where needed, particularly with your ELLs.

4   Ask for volunteers to share what, if anything, they've added.

5   Reread aloud Terkel's (1980) piece on Ben Green. Point out how dialogue or actually having someone speak can help make a vignette more lively and interesting. Use your own revised vignette as an example. Following is my example:

> "Working the Night Shift"
>
> I'd shuffle in with the others in a long, ragged column to the time clock. We'd punch in with two minutes to spare.
>   "Man, I didn't think I'd make it tonight," I said. "I'm so tired."
>   Usually I'd work with Betty and Slim, putting silver washers and nuts on auto gauges for ten hours with overtime.
>   "Who ever thought I'd spend my life handling nuts," Slim laughed.
>   In the din of the beveling presses pounding out the gauges I'd dream of a life somewhere out West, maybe the New Mexican desert with its turquoise sky and smell of pines.

6   Ask students to look at their vignettes and see where they might be able to add dialogue in order to make them livelier. (If your students have been keeping conversation journals and daily observation journals, this is a good time to suggest that they "mine" them for words, phrases, or interesting expressions.) Once again, assist where needed.

7   Ask for volunteers to share their expanded vignettes. Here's Dan's:

> I worked at Kowalski's for 3 years, 2 weeks and 3 days. I was a dishwasher. I took too many smoke breaks and got fired.
>   "You smoke too much," the boss said.
>   I moved on to F.R.B. Dining as a dishwasher. I got fired for fighting with another worker. I was there for 3 months, 2 weeks, and 4 days.
>   I hate dishwashing.

Once students have second drafts that they like and want to preserve as final drafts they can begin to look at spelling, grammar, and punctuation. (We'll work more with the mechanics of writing in Chapter 7.)

KEEPING ELLs IN MIND

1 Stephen Krashen (1982) observes that "conversation with someone who is interested in interacting with you, and who is trying to help you understand what he is saying, is good for second language acquisition" (p. 163). Thus, sharing work stories between an ELL and an interested native English speaker is one of the best prewriting activities in which you can have your ELLs engage.

2 If necessary, use an LEA format for those ELLs whose English writing skills are not yet adequate to capture their work stories. You or one of your more capable English-speaking students can serve as a scribe.

3 The reporter's 5Ws & H is a viable structure or format to promote with your ELLs. It gives them ready access to formulaic questions and phrases they can use both in speech and writing (just as in my very limited Spanish I first learned ¿Quién? ¿Qué? ¿Dónde? ¿Cuándo? ¿Por qué? and ¿Cómo?).

WRAP UP

1 In this lesson we've introduced prose vignettes, the reporter's 5Ws & H, revision, use of dialogue, and the importance of paying attention to particulars in writing through the notion of "appreciations." Once adults begin to write vignettes they discover that they can be used to write about almost anything in their lives; and they come to realize that writing can be a means of personal expression, pride, and power. It is vitally important to help adults develop this power, for as Deborah Brandt (2001) discovered in her longitudinal study, "across the generations, school-based writing was widely associated with pain, belittlement, and perplexity" (p. 164).

2 This lesson highlighted expressive writing, that is, writing that is closest to us. In the following lessons on prose vignettes we will explore poetic, expressive, and poetic/transactional forms of writing.

Vignettes About People and Things

This lesson highlights the fact that writing can be about anything, even the most commonplace things in our lives. We don't have to write about "big" ideas (although there is nothing wrong with that at times). Prose vignettes are ideally suited for this kind of writing. We can capture in print particular people, animals, or objects. Our writing can be humorous or serious. The vignette might be a piece of poetic discourse or it might be more of an expressive form of writing. You and your students have countless options here. The following examples are generally poetic forms of discourse that tell stories and describe in some detail either an animal or an object.

BEFORE THE LESSON

1   Read through the complete lesson and estimate how long it might take with your particular group of students. Determine if any of your ELLs will need additional assistance.

2   Make copies of "Timothy," written by an Adult Basic English student named Tom, for all students.

> I had a dog twenty-three years ago when I was eight. It was a smart dog. It did everything. We didn't have to teach it anything. Every time we threw a rock, he ran back to us.
>
> My dog's name was Timothy. He was a smart dog. We fed him a whole lot. We walked him around the block. Timothy was a girl dog. She used to have around twelve puppies. We gave away the puppies.
>
> One time I came home from school and asked my mother, "Where did the dog go?" Every time we'd come home from school the dog would be waiting on us. Momma said, "The dog man came and got him."
>
> We couldn't find out where he went because they had a lot of animal shelters there. They must have put him to sleep. I was very sad.

3   Write your own vignette that describes some object and make copies for your students. Here's mine as an example. I titled it "Watchbands."

> Leather watchbands have kept my pulse above the wrist on my left arm for how many years and for how many bands in the years? I've lost count, but I remember particular places and people.
>
> There was the toothless babushka that sold me a brown shoe leather-like band at a market stall in Odessa, Ukraine along with a kilo of dried Turkish apricots covered with white worms.
>
> A boy on the street in Accra, Ghana told me the band was genuine Moroccan leather, but when it broke in two the following month I found at its core pressed cardboard.
>
> Then there was the pretty teenager in the Seattle mall who sold me the most expensive kind by playing on my age with her smile.
>
> Watchbands don't only hold time, they also tell stories.

THE LESSON, PART I

1   Briefly explain your plans for the lesson.

2   Distribute copies of "Timothy" and have the students follow along as you read it. Reread the vignette and ask the students to read with you. Then have partners read it together. Match your ELLs with native English speakers.

3   Ask the students what they think about the vignette. I usually get responses that include: "It's a sad story", "I wonder if the mother wanted to get rid of the dog," and "That reminds me of my pets...."

4 After everyone has had a chance to share their reactions to the *content* of the vignette, ask your students to look again at the piece from a writer's perspective. What makes the piece work, and what might have made it stronger? I typically get responses that include: "It has a beginning, middle, and end," "It uses dialogue," and "It shows action." If no one comments, you should point out that more specifics would have made this piece more vivid, for example, by describing the kind of dog (a black Lab, German Shepherd, and so on), and by locating the story in a particular place (Seattle, Minneapolis, and so forth). Ask the students if they can think of any additional words or phrases that would make the vignette more descriptive, and to share these.

5 Explain to your students that this is an example of a prose vignette about an animal. Explain that vignettes can be about anything. They might simply describe something in detail or they might both describe and tell a story as "Timothy" does.

6 Distribute copies of your object vignette and read it aloud. Then have the students read it with you a second time.

7 Follow the same process that you used with "Timothy," that is, get students' reactions to the content and then have them explore the piece from their perspectives as writers. Reactions to my "Watchbands" piece have included such things as "The boy could be described," "What did the pretty teenager look like?" and "What kind of watch is it?"

8 Brainstorm as a whole class possible topics for a vignette. Encourage students to think about any person, animal, or object about which they might like to write. Stress that these objects can be as simple and seemingly insignificant as they might appear at first glance. Generate a long list on chart paper or the dry-erase board. (I recommend chart paper because the list might then be saved for future writing.) Here is part of a typical list generated by one group of students.

Owl candle

Powder horn

Coke bottle

Scuba gear

Blond girlfriend

Maroon Voyager

Juke boxes of the '50s

President of the United States

Half-ton Ford pickup truck

Nursing home

Sons and daughters

Bruce Springsteen

Aretha Franklin

9 Ask students to select one thing from the list (or something else that might come to mind while writing). In their writing notebooks or on loose sheets of paper have them brainstorm words, phrases, and ideas about the selected topic. Circulate among the students and offer assistance when needed.

10 Once they have brainstormed lists, model for your students by showing them how you used the 5Ws & H to generate ideas for your object vignette. Here's mine for "Watchbands."

> Who: I (Francis), different people who sold me bands, pretty teenager, old toothless woman, street kid
>
> What: leather watchbands worn over the years
>
> Where: different places; Ghana, Odessa, Seattle, mall, marketplace, on the street
>
> When: while teaching in different places, Odessa in 1992, Ghana in 1993, traveling in Washington in 2002
>
> Why: watchband worn out, cracked, broken
>
> How: bought the watchbands in different places, used different forms of currency, pretty teenager flirted and got me to buy an expensive band

11 Now ask your students to rearrange their brainstormed lists using the reporter's 5Ws & H as a structure.

12 Ask for a volunteer to share his brainstormed list using some or all of the 5Ws & H. As an example here's one from a student named Jeff.

> Who: Jeff
>
> What: Rod Carew Coke bottle
>
> Where: at Kowalski's, Minneapolis, in the pop section
>
> When: one day in the 1990s
>
> Why: Rod Carew was one of my favorite Twins players, it might be worth money some day, Rod in the Hall of Fame
>
> How: paid 59 cents for it

13 Have partners share their lists. During the sharing, other ideas might come up. Tell the students to add any new words, phrases, or ideas to their lists.

14 After students have shared and perhaps expanded their brainstormed lists, have them try a first draft of their object, person, or animal vignette. Encourage them to be as descriptive as possible and not to worry about spelling, and so forth. (Have your sticky notes ready for those students who balk at words they can't spell.) Circulate and assist where needed. Use an LEA approach if necessary with your ELLs.

15 Ask for one or two volunteers who would like to share their first drafts. Here's Jeff's:

> One day I was shopping at Kowalski's and found the Rod Carew Coke bottle in the pop section. I bought one for 59 cents and brought it home and drank it.
> I saved it because it might be worth some money some day, and Rod Carew is in the Hall of Fame.

Offer and encourage appreciations for the shared first drafts.

16 Have your students put away their first drafts until the next meeting (once again modeling the importance of incubation time for most pieces of writing).

THE LESSON, PART 2

1 Have students reread their first drafts, and then have them share with a new partner (not the one with whom they first shared the draft). During the sharing, other ideas might come up. Tell the students to add any new words, phrases, or ideas to their lists.

2 Model for students one aspect of the craft of writing. Tell them we can usually improve a piece of writing by looking at it again to see what we might add to make it stronger. Use your own vignette as an example. Here's mine with two additions in bold. They are based on the feedback from students in the first part of the lesson.

> Leather watchbands have kept my pulse above the wrist on my left arm for how many years and for how many bands in the years? I've lost count, but I remember peculiar places and people.
> There was the toothless babushka that sold me a brown shoe leather-like band at a market stall in Odessa, Ukraine along with a kilo of dried Turkish apricots covered with white worms.
> A **raggedly dressed** boy on the street in Accra, Ghana told me the band was genuine Moroccan leather, but when it broke in two the following month I found at its core pressed cardboard.
> Then there was the pretty **blue-eyed** teenager **with full lips and small white teeth** in the Seattle mall who sold me the most expensive kind by playing on my age with her smile.
> Watchbands don't only hold time, they also tell stories.

3 Ask students to add at least one thing (word or phrase) to their vignettes in order to make them more descriptive, lively, or clear. Have them work with a partner if they choose. Circulate and help when needed.

4 Ask for volunteers to share their revised vignettes. Offer and encourage appreciations from other students. Here's Jeff's revised vignette, with changes in bold:

> One day I was shopping at Kowalski's **in Minneapolis** and found the Rod Carew Coke bottle in the pop section. I bought one for 59 cents and brought it home and drank it.

I saved it because it might be worth some money some day, and Rod Carew is in the Hall of Fame.

5 If students are happy with their revised drafts, encourage them to begin working on a final copy.

KEEPING ELLs IN MIND

1 The same considerations I outlined in the previous vignette lesson apply here, that is, the importance of ELLs engaging in conversation with interested native English speakers, the use of LEA when needed, and the promotion of the reporter's 5Ws & H as a generative structure to use in a variety of spoken and written contexts.

2 This lesson incorporates the commonly used strategy of sentence expansion. It is an appropriate place for ELLs to consult reference books such as a simplified thesaurus for synonyms and new words in English.

WRAP UP

1 This lesson highlighted poetic writing, that is, writing concerned with the *made* object, the creative work.

2 The lesson helps adult students to think of themselves as writers and of writing as a craft. Too often adults who have not been successful in school perceive writing as something mysterious or something they cannot do. By engaging them in vignette writing about common things from their own lives and experiences, that is, objects, people, and so on, they see that writing can be about anything. By encouraging them to do what other professional writers often do, that is, make notes and lists, use some kind of organizational structure (5Ws & H), reflect and revise, they will begin to think of themselves as competent language users with something unique to say in writing. This is the kind of developmental approach to literacy that will help adults empower themselves personally, socially, and perhaps, politically.

Vignettes About Things of the Spirit

The prominent literacy historian Harvey Graff (1995) observes that "the significant link between literacy and religion forms one of the most vital, if (often but not always) conservative, legacies" of literacy in the West (p. 17). In her study of literacy in African American lives, Deborah Brandt (2001) found that there was at times an "intersection of the spiritual and the secular [that] arose in the inspirational writing and reading" of various individuals (p. 119). Victoria Purcell-Gates and Robin Waterman (2000) describe a finding of their literacy work with peasant women in El Salvador, "that one of the most important desires held by almost every student was to be able to read the Bible" (p. 83). Elizabeth Tisdell (1999) maintains that adult educators should understand that a "search for or an acknowledgement of the spiritual in the lives of adult learners is connected to how we create meaning in our relationships with others" (p. 93).

In my own work with adults of all ages, I have found that religion or things of the spirit are centrally important in the lives of many people. The Bible has been foremost among the various "authentic" texts that they wanted to read. (I have lived and taught mostly in communities where Christianity is the predominant religion.) A typical comment over the years is what a student once said to me: "Frank, I know the Scriptures by heart, but I want to be able to read the Word myself." Thus, as educators working with adults who have various reasons for wanting to improve their literacy abilities, I believe it is important that we think seriously about ways of incorporating things of the spirit into our lessons: "Being students of stories of faith and religion doesn't mean that we become proselytizers or that we ignore the differences between public and religious education. It simply means honoring the complexity of life" (Kazemek, 2002b, p. 380).

This prose vignette lesson highlights writing that tends to be expressive in nature but, quite often, reflects aspects of poetic discourse.

BEFORE THE LESSON

1 Informally through discussion gain an understanding of your students' religious beliefs and practices (if any). Ask if they have any favorite books or texts that they hold dear, like to hear, or like to read. Ask if they would bring in favorites. (If you don't have much of a background in a set of particular beliefs, ask your students for help and do a little background reading on your own. I've had to do this with Islam.)

2 Read through the complete lesson and estimate how long it might take with your particular group of students. Decide if any of your ELLs will need additional assistance.

3 Locate one or more (depending upon your group of students and their beliefs and practices) of your favorite spiritual texts. As an example, following is a well-known passage, Ecclesiastes 3, 1–8, from *The Holy Bible, King James Version* (1971) that I have often used:

> To every thing there is a season, and a time to every purpose under heaven: A time to be born, and a time to die; A time to plant, and a time to pluck up that which is planted; A time to kill, and a time to heal; a time to break down, and a time to build up; A time to weep, and a time to laugh; a time to mourn, and a time to dance; A time to cast away stones, and a time to gather stones together; a time to embrace, and a time to refrain from embracing; A time to get, and a time to lose; a time to keep, and a time to cast away; A time to rend, and a time to sew; a time to keep silence, and a time to speak; A time to love, and a time to hate; a time of war, and a time of peace. (p. 612)

I prefer the King James Version to various modern translations. This verse is widely known (individuals and groups have recorded musical versions of it over the decades) and contains simple but "rich" language. The parallel structure and use of repetition make it easy to read for even the most beginning readers and writers.

4 Write your own prose vignette based upon the model or models you use with your students. Make copies for all students. Here's mine as an example:

> There is a time for all kinds of writing and reading: A time to write journals, and a time to write stories; A time to read comic strips, and a time to read novels; A time to write grocery lists, and a time to write vignettes; A time to read work manuals, and a time to read poetry; A time to write business letters, and a time to write love letters; A time to read recipes, and a time to read prayers.

THE LESSON, PART I

1 Briefly explain your plans for the lesson.

2 Share the religious or spiritual text that you've decided to use. (If you are using texts from different traditions, share them over several days or weeks. Don't overload your students with too many new texts at one time.) I'm basing this lesson on Ecclesiastes 3, 1–8, in the King James Version of the Bible. Have the students follow along as you read it. Reread the vignette and ask the students to read with you. Then have partners read it together. Match your ELLs with native English speakers.

3 Encourage a whole-class discussion of the vignette. Ecclesiastes has generated such typical comments as "That's the truth, you can't always be happy," "It seems like there's more war than peace," and "Isn't that the way life is?"

4 Explore with students the structure of the vignette, that is, the use of contrasts, parallel structure, and repetition. Share your vignette and describe how you developed it. Make a list on the dry-erase board or chart paper to demonstrate how you brainstormed and did a form of note taking. Here's what I did with mine.

Reading	Writing
Time for:	
comic strips & novels	journals & stories
work manuals & poetry	grocery lists & vignettes
recipes & prayers	business letters & love letters

5 Brainstorm and list possible contrasts for different vignettes based on Ecclesiastes. Encourage a wide range of possibilities. For example, my vignette might not appear to be particularly "spiritual," but I always point out to students that I believe reading and writing can be spiritual and even holy acts.

6 After the class brainstorming and listing, have individuals develop their own lists. Assist ELLs or have them work with a native English-speaking partner.

7 Ask one or more volunteers to share their lists. Here's a partial list from a woman named Gertrude:

happy/sad

laugh/cry

work/play

talk/listen

shout/listen

eat/diet

sin/repent

8 Instruct students to reflect on their lists before the next class meeting and to add new ideas to their lists. Encourage them to talk with their family members, friends, fellow religious community members, or spiritual advisors. (You might have students try a first draft here, but I have found that waiting until students have had time for reflection and talk with others before writing results in richer texts.)

THE LESSON, PART 2

1 Review from the first part of the lesson. Reread Ecclesiastes and then do a choral reading with the whole class: you read the first part of each statement (A time to be born), and have the students read the second part in response (and a time to die). You might also divide the class in two and then have a second choral reading. (I have found that students like to listen to the Byrds' version titled "Turn, turn, turn." If you have access to that recording or subscribe to a service such as iTunes, I urge you to use it.)

2 Have students review their brainstormed lists of contrasts from the last meeting. Ask if anyone has gotten any new ideas. Encourage volunteers to share. Tell individuals to add to their lists anything they hear from others that they also might like to consider.

3 Ask students to begin writing their own vignettes based on Ecclesiastes. Tell them to refer to their brainstormed lists and the ideas shared in the whole class discussions. Circulate and assist when needed, perhaps by helping ELLs through LEA, helping certain individuals move ahead by providing them with correct spellings on sticky notes, and helping individuals who seem to be "stuck" and simply can't begin their vignette.

4 Once students have a first draft or have at least started on a first draft (of course, the specific amount of time you allow for writing will depend upon your particular situation and students), ask for volunteers to share. Here as an example is the final version of Gertrude's vignette.

As a person goes through life certain situations present themselves from time to time: A time to be happy, and a time to be sad; A time to laugh, and a time to cry; A time to gather, and a time to scatter that which was gathered; A time to work, and a time to play; A time to walk, and a time to ride; A time to talk, and a time to listen; A time to shout, and a time to whisper; A time to mend, and a time to rip that which was mended; A time to sit, and a time to stand; A time to sleep, and a time to be awake; A time to exercise, and a time to relax; A time to eat, and a time to diet; A time to sin, and a time to repent the sin.

5 After volunteers have shared, ask them to put away their first drafts for further incubation. Return to them in subsequent meetings and help students shape them into final, edited versions with correct spelling and punctuation.

KEEPING ELLs IN MIND

Writing vignettes about things of the spirit or religious beliefs and practices gives your ELLs an opportunity to express something about themselves and their culture that they typically have little opportunity to do in educational settings. Jack Cassidy and colleagues' (2004) study of a successful family literacy program for Latino parents and caregivers highlights the importance of respecting and valuing the participants' culture. Moreover, such writing typically fosters new awareness and learning.

WRAP UP

1 In her study of how adults know the world in different ways and how those ways of knowing affect teaching and learning, Eleanor Drago-Severson (2004) maintains that regardless of the differences among adults in terms of how they construct knowledge, "it is developmentally helpful when instructors can relate assignments to learners' life experiences" (p. 161). And as I stress in this lesson, for many adults religion, religious practices, prayer, and things of the spirit are central to their life experiences. As literacy educators we ignore these things to the detriment of our students' learning and our own meaningful practice. As I've written in the past, "If literacy education isn't grounded in the particular, then it's useless, little more than indoctrination or training for the menial" (Kazemek, 1998, p. 59).

2 Little booklets of students' final drafts of these Ecclesiastes vignettes along with other similar kinds of spiritual or meditative writings (for example, topics that I have found viable include "forks in life's road," "mother's/father's/child's love," "helping others," "forgiveness," and "accepting difference") can be assembled and used for further reading and particular skills instruction. Such booklets also have helped form a bridge between the literacy classroom and the rest of the community; individuals have shared them with family members, friends, and ministers.

Oral History Vignettes About Other People

In the introduction to his collection of oral histories, *Hope Dies Last: Keeping Faith in Difficult Times*, oral historian Studs Terkel (2003) observes,

As we enter the new millennium, hope appears to be an American attribute that has vanished for many, no matter what their class or condition in life. The official word has never been more arrogantly imposed. Passivity, in the face of such a bold, unabashed show of power from above, appears to be the order of the day. But it ain't necessarily so. (p. xv)

Similarly, in adult literacy education "it ain't necessarily so" that adults must passively accept whatever "best practices" curriculum someone imposes on them (Velazquez, 1996). Interviewing others and writing about other people's lives helps adults become active users of language and involved members of their community.

In his book on oral history, Ken Howarth (1998) maintains that oral history promotes "speaking, and listening, writing and an awareness of the richness of language, including dialect and other non-standard English" (p. 95). Modeling for adults how to interview others and then how to shape those interviews into written prose vignettes is the purpose of this lesson. In a real sense oral history interviewing and writing helps adults play in James Britton's (1982) universe of discourse by using language in the role of a "participant" when interviewing someone and then in the role of a "spectator" when shaping that interview into an engaging text for others to read; in Britton's terms it allows adults to explore both "transactional" and "poetic" writing.

This lesson is structured around a basic format that Helen Woodrow and I presented in 2001 (Woodrow & Kazemek, 2001): Explore a topic, rehearse in class, interview in the community, work with the interview data, and publish the oral history vignettes.

BEFORE THE LESSON

1 Read through the complete lesson and estimate how long it might take with your group of students. Consider any special adaptations you might have to make for your ELLs.

2 Go to the StoryCorps homepage (www.storycorps.net) and spend some time exploring the site. Listen to a number of the interviews. StoryCorps is a national project that instructs and inspires individuals to record one another's stories. There are a number of StoryCorps booths around the United States (the first in New York City), mobile booths that move from region to region, and plans for booths in public libraries. The interviews are regularly aired on National Public Radio, and all of them are housed at the Library of Congress. The goal is to develop an oral history of America. The StoryCorps homepage contains scores of interview excerpts that are approximately two to three minutes in length. You can access them by categories such as Growing Up, Work, Friendship, Wisdom, Struggle, and so forth. The interviewers and interviewees represent all walks of life, ages, and racial/ethnic backgrounds. These brief interview excerpts provide wonderful models for adult students. Moreover, 49 of the StoryCorps interviews have been edited and collected in *Listening Is an Act of Love: A Celebration of American Life From the StoryCorps Project* (Isay, 2007).

3 Choose one or two selections that you think would be interesting to share with your group of students. For example, in the Wisdom category a nephew talks with his aunt in a heart-rending manner about being ridiculed because of his weight. In the Struggle category a grandfather describes to his grandson that while in the Navy he was denied admittance into a movie theater because he was black. And in Growing Up a father and his 15-year-old daughter with Down Syndrome share their feelings about family and love.

4 Use an audiotape recorder when you talk with a friend, neighbor, or someone in your community that you find interesting. Focus on one of the categories from StoryCorps. If you have not done much interviewing before, look at the guidelines for interviewing provided on the StoryCorps homepage or simply follow the simple process described in the lesson. (The purpose of this lesson is to get you and your students to write short oral history vignettes and not to turn all of you into oral historians—although that would indeed be wonderful!) Select a section from your audiotape and shape it into a brief vignette as a model for your students. Make copies for your students. Here is a vignette I wrote after interviewing a 90-year-old woman about where she was born and lived her whole life, in Minnesota.

> Can you tell me a little about when your family came into this area?

> "My Dad was a mechanic in a garage in a little town in Iowa, and he suffered from headaches quite a bit. He received an invitation from an old friend who was up here in Pine River [Minnesota]—of course it really wasn't Pine River then—to come up and see this part of the country.
>   "When Dad arrived there were blueberries, raspberries, wild strawberries; the red clover came up to his knees! All he had to do was to go behind his friend's barn and there was Norway Lake. It was easy to catch fish in those days. You really didn't have to use bait. You could put a little piece of paper on a hook, and they'd grab at it.
>   "It was all wonderful! Dad fell in love with the country and bought our farm."

5 Gather a number of audiotape recorders from your organization, public library, friends, or other sources. You should have one recorder for every three students.

THE LESSON, PART I

1 Explain to your students what they'll be doing in the lesson, that is, interviewing one another and then using those interviews to write oral history vignettes. Afterwards they might do the same with friends and people in their own communities.

2 Briefly describe the StoryCorps project and then play the excerpts that you se-lected. Stop after each one and elicit responses. Typically adults will make personal connections to the interviews. For example, the father and his 15-year-old daughter with Down Syndrome talked about family and love. I've had people comment: "My daughter has a child with Downs," or "It brought tears to my eyes when the daughter asks her father how he felt when she was born."

3 Play a few minutes of your recorded interview. Explain whom you talked with and how you went about it. Then distribute copies of your oral history vignette. Have the students follow along as you read it. Then read it a second time, encouraging the students to join in. Ask them to compare the recorded piece you played with the written version. If necessary, play the recording again. What you want to accomplish here is for your students to see that written language is more than simply "talk written down," and that writing oral history vignettes involves a *shaping* process on the part of the writer.

4 Ask your students to form partner teams. Be sure to match ELLs with native English speakers. Tell them you're going to give them three minutes each to interview their partner, and then the interviewee will become the interviewer for three minutes. (Three minutes for each person is plenty of time. If it goes longer, people often lose focus.) Have them ask their partners about a favorite, memorable, or special place in their lives; it might be a present place or something from the past. I've had people share such things as a marketplace in a Mexican border town, sledding hill from childhood, bedroom, backyard, grandparents' house, and so forth.

5 After partners have interviewed each other have the class share. Discuss any difficulties they might have had in getting a partner to talk, elaborate, and so forth. Tell them that the next part of the oral history process would be for them to write a short vignette capturing their partner's special or favorite place. Emphasize why an audio recording device is so important when interviewing someone: you can go back and listen again to the specifics of what a person said.

6 Tell your students that at the next meeting they'll be interviewing in small groups and then writing vignettes based on the interviews. Ask if any individuals have audio recording devices at home, and if they do would they be willing to bring them to the next class meeting along with tapes.

THE LESSON, PART 2

1 Review the last meeting, that is, features of the oral history interviews, the connections between listening to someone's oral story and then shaping it into a brief vignette, and the importance of people's everyday lives. I typically share once again a minute or two of my audiotaped interview and then read again the written vignette, for example the "falling in love with Pine River" piece described earlier.

2 Brainstorm with your students possible topics about which they'd like to interview one another. The StoryCorps categories are often useful here to stimulate topic ideas. You also might suggest, if necessary, some of the possible topics I mentioned at the beginning of this chapter, such as stories of work, "firsts," family members, and so forth. As the adults brainstorm, stress that oral history interviews don't have to be about grand events or things. List the topics on the dry-erase board or chart paper.

3 Once the adults have chosen a topic divide the class into groups of three. Be sure there is at least one native English speaker in each trio. I have found it best to have two people interview one, and that is true with children, adolescents, adults, or elders. Two students can support each other in terms of questioning, note taking, and so forth. Have each team decide who will be interviewed.

4 Using a volunteer, model for the class how you would go about the process. The reporter's 5Ws & H come into play here. Use open-ended questions (stressing the use of "Why?" and "Tell me more" as follow-ups to brief or one-word responses) and demonstrate how you take brief notes. It's best to spend time talking through the process as you demonstrate it. Tell them if you knew in advance whom you were going to interview you'd have prepared a few questions. (The StoryCorps website has a wealth of resources and possible questions.)

5 Distribute the recording devices, one to each group. Spend a few minutes having the students practice using the recorders by testing, adjusting volume, and locating the "stop," "play," and "pause" buttons. Most adults with whom I've worked have experience with audiotape recorders, and this doesn't take much time.

6 Tell the students to begin their interviews. Be sure that the teams are spread out around the classroom or even in another room in order to avoid interfering with one another. Tell them as they are recording their interviews one or both of the interviewers might want also to jot down any words, phrases, or expressions they think are interesting. Circulate amongst the teams and assist if needed.

7 These first interviews usually take 5 to 10 minutes. Once all of the teams have completed their interviews, debrief the process. Were there any difficulties? Did the audiotape recorders work? Did they have trouble coming up with questions?

8 Have the teams play back their tapes listening for the "rich" and interesting parts of the interviewee's story. While listening, tell them to note on the recording device's counter where those parts are in order to be able to go back and easily access them. Instruct them to also jot down any words, phrases or sentences that "grab" them, using the "pause" button as necessary.

9 Ask one of the teams to volunteer, and share what they have highlighted. As a whole class, brainstorm how the team might begin to shape what they've gathered from the recording and their notes into a short written vignette.

10 Have the teams select one piece of the interview that they want to now transform into a written vignette. Have them listen to that little section again and transcribe words, phrases, or even complete sentences. Tell them they should not try to write down *everything* from the recording. Stress again that they are *shaping* the interviewee's oral language into a written vignette by using parts of what he said. Be aware that this is usually the most difficult part of getting adults to engage in oral history and writing. Most people want to write down everything. Circulate and provide guidance and suggestions where needed.

11 When students have first drafts or parts of first drafts, ask each team to share what it has written up to that point in time. Here are a couple of examples on the topic of "Winter as Kids":

> We'd bundle up and take our sleds to the hill on the road to our aunt and uncle's house. One evening there was so much light from the full moon. It lit up the earth like day. The snow crackled under our boots....

> I used to walk at night in the snowdrifts with my dog. She always had a great time. The moon would be so light I could see rabbits hopping about. Sometimes I could hear the owls and their lonely sound....

12 Collect the drafts or make copies of them if you have ready access to a copy machine. Tell your students that they'll have time to work on them at the next meeting. Label the recordings and keep them until the next meeting.

THE LESSON, PART 3

1 Gather together the teams from the last meeting. (Quite often adults in literacy programs don't make every class session for any number of reasons. If that occurs try to rearrange the teams with at least one of the original members in each group. If students are absent, rearrange the trios as best you can. For example, you might have individuals from different teams working together on only one set of drafts and recordings.)

2 Distribute the drafts and recordings. Allow time for the teams to listen again to the recordings and to work on their drafts. Circulate and offer suggestions where needed.

3 Have each team share its oral history vignette. Encourage appreciations. Collect them for your final editing, typing, and copying. The students can then help assemble the oral history vignettes into booklets to be used for reading activities and as models for future vignette writing.

THE LESSON, PART 4

Depending upon your students' interest in oral history interviewing and writing, you can follow this process many times, helping them become more skilled questioners, note takers, and shapers of oral language—especially dialect and vernacular speech—into written texts. Oral history celebrates writing as a social process, validates adults' experiences, and helps them better understand what we mean by "voice." Moreover, by interviewing one another, adults not only help form a stronger classroom community but also foster an atmosphere of competence: *They* are the interviewers and not merely the responders to teachers' or workbooks' questions.

KEEPING ELLs IN MIND

1   Collaborative oral history interviewing and writing in the classroom provides many benefits for your ELLs. As Joy Kreeft Peyton (1993) observes, "The life experiences of many adults learning English as a second language (ESL) in this country can be particularly compelling.... At the same time, these stories can be a powerful learning tool for adults enrolled in ESL, literacy, and general education programs" (p. 59). ELLs' experiences are acknowledged and explored within the supportive context of a group of native speakers.

2   Listening to StoryCorps interviews online or on audiotapes or CDs you have prepared helps ELLs become more familiar with spoken vernacular English. They can listen at times in class or in the privacy of their own homes. This emphasis on listening helps keep Stephen Krashen's (1982) "affective filter" low.

3   The process of interviewing, note taking, and writing provides ELLs with opportunities to try out spoken English in a safe, supportive context. Their native English-speaking peers are able to clarify misunderstandings or answer questions about particular words. Moreover, ELLs are able to observe how native English speakers construct written texts.

4   The StoryCorps interviewing guidelines provide a wealth of questions that your ELLs can use to help develop their understanding and use of the interrogative in English, for example, What was the happiest moment of your life? The saddest? Who was the most important person in your life? Can you tell me about him or her? What are the most important lessons you've learned in life? Practice forming simple questions beginning with the 5Ws & H can be tied to the lesson on Writing Dramatic Scripts described in Chapter 6.

WRAP UP

1   Oral history interviewing and writing can be as limited or as expansive as you and your students choose to make it. The interviews can be limited to the classroom or they can be taken out into the community. Students can interview family members, friends, or others in their particular home environments. These interviews can be brought back into the classroom for further discussion, writing, vocabulary and grammar work, and for pleasure reading.

> By providing students with the appropriate structure, support, and practical skills, we can help them become the interviewers, recorders, and oral historians of their own communities. This will greatly enhance their literacy abilities and foster their sense of being literacy producers. (Woodrow & Kazemek, 2001, p. 3)

2   For those interested in pursuing the oral history process in depth, I suggest that you begin with the Woodrow and Kazemek (2001) overview available on the Internet at www.nald.ca/library/newsletter/naldnews/01winter/netfront.htm. Again,

the StoryCorps site offers great resources and ideas. In addition to Ken Howarth's (1998) book mentioned previously, Cynthia Stokes Brown's *Like It Was: A Complete Guide to Writing Oral History* (1988) is a rich resource for the nitty-gritty of doing oral history.

CHAPTER 3

Sparking Enthusiasm
With Poetry Writing

J OSEPH BRODSKY, the late Nobel Laureate, contended that everyone in some
fashion should be engaged in poetry writing:

> I think that a reader, lamentable though it may be, always lags severely behind. No matter how
> highly he thinks of himself, no matter how well he understands a given poet, nonetheless, sad
> though it is, he is always just a reader... When you compose a single line, things occur to you
> that in principle shouldn't. This is why you should be involved in literature. Why, ideally, *everyone*
> [emphasis in the original] should be involved in literature. It is a species-specific, biological neces-
> sity. The individual's duty to himself, to his own DNA. (as cited in Volkov, 1998, p. 127)

I love Brodsky's contention because it acknowledges the important connections between reading and writing, celebrates poetic literature, and affirms the fact that the
writing of poetry is not only for a select few. It is a biological necessity and a duty each
person owes to herself.

Why poetry? I have maintained elsewhere that the

> purpose of poetry is to enlarge our lives. It helps us see the world and other people in all their
> complexity and possibility.... Poetry also enlarges our lives through the pleasure it gives us and
> the joy and excitement we feel when we read it, hear it, talk about it, and relate it to our own
> lives. (Kazemek & Rigg, 1995, p. 15)

Naomi Shihab Nye says that poetry "is a conversation with the world; poetry is a conversation with the words on the page in which you allow those words to speak back to
you; and poetry is a conversation with yourself" (as cited in Moyers, 1995, p. 321).

Regardless of the age, gender, ethnicity, or literacy ability of the adults with whom
I've worked over the years, I have found that poetry is the one form of writing that almost
without exception everyone eventually engages in with enthusiasm. Of course, at first
many adults are reluctant to read or write poetry because of past negative experiences. "I
never understood it" and "I can't do that kind of thing" are typical comments. Once they
see that they *can* write poetry and take joy in what they have written, however, they are
eager to continue exploring different poetic forms. Indeed, if you take even a cursory look

at the various collections of writing by adult literacy students either published by local organizations or available on the Internet, you will see that a great deal of it is poetry.

In this chapter, I present five poetry lessons that encourage students (and their teachers) to write and become familiar with different types of poetry. These various poetic forms are easily accessible even to adults with limited literacy abilities and, with little practice, are simple to write (although the subject matter might be quite serious or complicated). The lessons explore lunes, cinquains and diamantes, bio-poems, apology poems, and poems from poems. Over the years I have had success with all of these forms. I believe that you will, too.

These lessons are built around a particular format, one that I have found beneficial for writing with people of all ages and of all abilities. Because many adults are afraid of poetry and likewise have seldom if ever written any poems, a supportive structure and modeling are of utmost importance. The general structure for writing poems with adults includes the following:

1. Reading to and with students examples of the particular type of poetry, including your own
2. Exploring the characteristics of the particular type
3. Brainstorming possible ideas
4. Writing one or more poems as a whole class
5. Sharing and discussing the class's poems
6. Writing one or more poems in partners or small groups
7. Sharing the partner or small-group poems
8. Writing poems individually
9. Sharing individual poems
10. Writing, editing, and collecting of individual poems

Lunes

A lune is a three-line poem that can reflect any mood and be about any topic. It is a cousin to the haiku and much more natural to write. There is no artificial syllable counting, and thus the writer is concerned solely with making something interesting with words. Because lunes are short, they are appealing to adults with limited experience or writing ability. They are an especially viable form of writing for ELLs. Moreover, once adults gain confidence writing lunes, they readily share them with their children and often continue to compose them with their children at home.

A lune is a three-line poem of 11 words:

• First line: three words
• Second line: five words
• Third line: three words

Following is a lune I wrote:

> A sparrow clings
> to the window screen while
> I sit reading

A lune might take the form of a single sentence (as in the previous example) or it might simply be a set of images, for example this autumn lune I wrote:

> Golden maple leaves
> crab apples hanging on branches
> wooly worms crawl

Punctuation might be used (as in capitalization of the first word or the first word of each line) or it might not. The important thing is to have students focus on creating something poetic with language. Word choice, images, and sound are important (as they are important with all poetry). Writing lunes encourages students to explore words and accordingly helps them to expand their reading and writing vocabularies.

BEFORE THE LESSON

1 Read through the complete lesson and estimate how long it might take with your particular group of students. Decide if any of your ELLs will need additional assistance.

2 Write a number of lunes in order to understand how the form works and to spark your own creativity and joy of language. The more the better, but try to write at least a dozen. You'll find that once you get going it's hard to stop! Moreover, you want to have plenty of examples for your students. The top two examples are my own and the bottom two examples are by my colleague, Jerry.

The dark water in the bird bath mirrors a lone goldfinch	A loon pair teaching young how to fish eagle circling overhead
muddy shoes again the prints of country living follow me around	Chicago is sinking subsiding one millimeter per year are you concerned

3 Make copies for the students of your lunes (and perhaps those written by other people, with permission; you may use the ones here as possible examples).

4 Gather a collection of colorful pictures or photographs. I like to use pictures of nature (animals, insects, flowers, trees, and so on) that I've collected from such magazines as *National Geographic*, *Nature*, *Discovery*, and from the magazine section of the Sunday newspaper.

THE LESSON

1 Distribute the copies to your students. Have them follow along as you read two or three of your lunes. Read each one at least twice or even three times. (It is vital that *all* poetry be read *aloud* at least twice! Poetry must be *heard*; it's an oral art form as well as a written one. As the poet Donald Hall (1993) remarks, "If we try reading poetry with our eyes, as we learn to read newspapers, we miss its bodiliness as well as the history bodied into its words" (p. 8).

2 Ask partners to read the lunes together and then to read them individually to each other. Finally read them as a whole class in a choral manner. Clarify any unusual words or phrases that you might have used.

3 Encourage reactions and discussion of the lunes. Again, my prompt is, "What do you think about it?" You will most likely get comments about the content of the poems ("The eagle is threatening the loon babies." "Is Chicago really sinking?") and about the form ("Why isn't there any punctuation at the end?" "Why aren't words capitalized?").

4 Explain to students that the poems are a particular form called lune. On the dry-erase board or chart paper write *Lune* and then write *Loon*. Distinguish between the spellings and tell them that the first one is the poem and the second is the water bird. Ask the students to look at their copies of the lunes and to see if they can tell what the form of the poem is. (You might get several different responses, for example, "it's short," but after some exploration and discussion students will observe that a lune has three lines with three words in the first, five in the second, and three in the last.)

Select one of the pictures and pass it around for all students to examine. (If you have access to an overhead projector or computer projection setup, you might display it in that manner.) As a whole class, brainstorm ideas about the picture. Tell students to examine the picture closely and to also think about those things that the picture triggers in their memories. Make a list on the dry-erase board or chart paper. Here's part of a brainstormed list about a picture of an orange grove.

oranges	growing
trees	fruit
California	look like lemons
Florida	cool drink
juicy	healthy
thick skin	harvest
beautiful	migrant workers
juice	picking

5 Once you have a substantial list ask for volunteers to begin the first line of a lune. Write the ideas on the dry-erase board or chart paper. As the students compose the lune, read and reread each line in an LEA manner while pointing to each word as you read it the first time and then running your fingers under each line on subsequent readings. (That way you highlight the individual words as well as larger chunks of language.) After students have composed a lune, read it as a whole class.

6 Tell students that from the picture and the brainstormed list they can usually write several, if not many, lunes. Follow the same process and as a class write two or three more about the picture. Here are three that students composed on the orange grove:

> oranges growing on
> California and Florida fruit trees
> they are beautiful
>
> juicy cool oranges
> picked by poor migrant workers
> in hot Florida
>
> orange juice is
> healthy for children and adults
> a cool drink

7 After the class has composed several lunes on the particular picture, clarify any doubts, misgivings, or misunderstandings the students might have. For example, students might object that "these don't look or sound like poems," "they don't rhyme," and so forth. Highlight the fact that there are many different types of poetry, and that all poems don't have to rhyme, but some indeed do.

8 Distribute the photographs to partners. Give each partner team at least five photographs from which they might choose to write. Tell them to follow the same process as in the whole-class composition. Match any ELLs with native English speakers as you circulate and assist where necessary.

9 After partners have written drafts of one or more lunes, share them among the whole class. Ask if there were any problems writing the lunes and, once again, clarify any misunderstandings. (A not unusual question revolves around the 3-5-3-word pattern. Sometimes students will come up with a lune that has a 4-5-3, 3-6-3, or other pattern and they'll want to know if that's "OK." Tell them it is. Stress that they're writing poetry, and making a poem is more important than sticking strictly to the form.)

10 At this point depending upon the amount of time you have, students as individuals might try their hands at writing their own lunes. If they are not comfortable doing so, let them continue working as partners.

11 Ask students to write several lunes before the next class meeting. They might take one or more of your pictures or they might use pictures or photographs that they have at home. Tell them that they don't necessarily have to use pictures though; lunes can be written about anything—objects, people, places, and so on.

KEEPING ELLs IN MIND

1 Writing lunes is a productive and generative activity for ELLs. They are not restricted by grammar, punctuation, or spelling. The focus is on vocabulary and meaning. Even with a small stock of English vocabulary (whether from their journals, other texts, or other people) they can compose these little poems. Moreover, lunes also allow ELLs to play around with multiple-meaning words (for example, *bear*) and homophones (for example, *loon* and *lune*). Following is an example of a playful poem written by an ELL and her native English-speaking partner:

> This lune is
> about a water bird that
> we call loon.

2 I have found it best to begin writing poetry of any kind as partners or in trio groupings. As I've mentioned, most adults, regardless of their educational backgrounds and literacy abilities, are tentative when asked to write poetry. It's important to put them at ease and give them the support of their peers (and thus lower the "affective filter"). This is especially true for ELLs.

WRAP UP

1 Share the individually written lunes when students return to class. Highlight the variety among the writers. For example, Glen wrote, "Don't be a/fool and jump out of school/stay in strong." (In this particular poem students can see how rhyme might be used even with lunes.) Assist students with spelling and punctuation on final drafts.

2 Encourage students to write at least one lune a week. (I tell them that I try to write a poem a day, however brief.) Suggest that those with children write some as a family activity. Brief sharing of lunes (and other poems) is a great way to begin each class session.

3 Once students have written a number of lunes that they like, you and they can assemble the poems into a booklet to be shared with others, reread, and used perhaps for particular skills instruction.

Cinquains and Diamantes

Cinquains and diamantes are also form poems that follow particular patterns. They are easy to write and widely used with students of all ages. I have found them particularly useful when writing with adults, especially those with limited literacy abilities or with limited English-language skills. Because they highlight different kinds of words and not sentences, students don't have to worry about punctuation and grammar. Moreover, you as a teacher can use them to highlight specific kinds of language, for example, nouns, verbs, and so forth.

A cinquain is a five-line poem that follows a particular pattern.

- First line: one word, the subject or the title of the poem
- Second line: two words (adjectives), describe the first line
- Third line: three words (participles), describe actions of the subject in the first line
- Fourth line: four words (that might be a phrase or sentence), that express a feeling you have about the subject or that the subject has about itself
- Fifth line: one word, another name for the subject in the first line; it might be literal or figurative

Here's an example by Joanne:

> Snow
> white beautiful
> covering beautifying exhilarating
> drifts are a challenge
> sliding

And here's an example by a group of adult students:

> Working
> necessary enjoyable
> living struggling surviving
> fun if on time
> again

A diamante is a seven-line poem that is built around the cinquain. It begins with one subject and moves to its opposite or to some new subject.

- First line: one word, the subject or the title of the poem
- Second line: two words (adjectives), describe the first line
- Third line: three words (participles), describe actions of the subject in the first line
- Fourth line: four words (any kind) in which the first two relate to the subject of line 1 and the last two relate to the subject in line 7
- Fifth line: three words (participles), describe actions of the subject in the last line
- Sixth line: two words (adjectives) describe the last line

• Seventh line: the new subject that is opposite or somehow different from that of the first line

Following is an example that I wrote after an intergenerational writing project in which a group of 18-year-olds interviewed and wrote with a group of elders.

> Oak
> Rooted weathered
> Sheltering showering blessing
> Acorns fall seedlings rise
> Reaching spreading swaying
> Hopeful tender
> Oak

When writing a diamante the first thing you do is to write the first and last lines. This provides the structure of the poem stating the opposites or subject you are moving from and the subject to which you are moving in the poem. In this case I use *oak* for both lines because I want to show metaphorically how the old oak trees (elders) produce and sustain the young oak trees (the 18-year-olds). The second and third lines are those of a cinquain. The fourth line is the pivot point of the diamante. In it you begin to move from the subject of the first line (in this case the oaks as elders) to the subject of the last line (that is, the oaks as youthful). Typically we do this by referring to the subject in the first line with the first two words and the subject of the last line with the next two words. Lines five, six, and seven are simply an inverted cinquain relating to the subject in the last line.

BEFORE THE LESSON

1 Read through the complete lesson and estimate how long it might take with your particular group of students. Decide if any of your ELLs will need additional assistance.

2 This lesson will take at least two, but most likely more, sessions. During the first lesson you will introduce the cinquain and write some with your students. Once they are comfortable writing cinquains, you will introduce the diamante as an extension and then write some with your class.

3 Write a number of cinquains and diamantes in order to understand how the forms work and to spark your own creativity and joy of language. Try to write at least a half-dozen or so of each; the more the better.

4 Make copies of your cinquains and diamantes for your students. Be sure to include the directions for each line as I explained earlier.

THE LESSON, PART I

1 Distribute copies of one or two of your cinquains to the students. Have them follow along as you read. Once again, read each one at least twice or even three times.

2 On the dry-erase board or chart paper, show students the format of the cinquain. (If you think it is appropriate for your particular group of students, you might use the technical terms of *noun*, *adjective*, and so on. But be careful, your primary purpose is to engage students in poetry writing and not to teach directly the parts of speech.)

3 Brainstorm with your students possible topics about which to write one or more cinquains. Tell them it is always best to have present the thing you're writing about; that way you can examine it and get ideas. You might suggest objects in the classroom, for example, a clock, water or soda bottle, shirt or blouse, fast-food container, snack package, and so forth.

4 Once the class has decided on a particular object, brainstorm possible words and ideas relating to it. List them on the dry-erase board or chart paper.

5 Following the cinquain format, encourage volunteers to suggest ideas for each line. I find it useful to demonstrate that it's easy to write cinquains by having the students write two cinquains at the same time from their brainstormed list. For example, here are two class cinquains written from the same list:

McDonald's	McDonald's
Delicious cheap	Fat unhealthy
Frying tasting munching	Salting ketchuping loving
There is nothing better	I love them so
Big Mac	Fries

6 After you and the students have written several cinquains as a whole class, ask partners to write one or more from the list of possible subjects or from new ideas they generate. Circulate and assist where needed. This is an especially appropriate time to introduce and encourage students to use such basic reference sources as a thesaurus. Thesauri are written at all levels of complexity, and inexpensive paperback editions are readily available.

7 After partners have written one or more cinquains, have volunteers share. Offer appreciations and encourage others to do so. Answer questions and clarify any misunderstandings, particularly the notion that one *must* adhere to the specific line format. Emphasize that it's OK to change the 1-2-3-4-1 format if that results in a better poem.

8 If there's time, have individuals try their hands at one or more cinquains. Assist with an LEA approach for those students who might need such help.

9 If time allows, have one or more individuals share their drafts.

10 Ask students to write some cinquains at home before the next class meeting. Encourage them to write at least three. Tell them to look about their homes and write about whatever grabs their fancy.

THE LESSON, PART 2

1 Share cinquains that your students and you have written. Review the basic 1-2-3-4-1 structure of the cinquain.

2 Distribute copies of the diamantes you and perhaps others have written. (You may use the examples in the previous section if you'd like.) On the dry-erase board or chart paper explain the basic structure of a diamante by relating it to the cinquain. Stress the importance of beginning with the first and last lines.

3 Brainstorm with students possible topics or contrasts about which you might write a whole-class diamante and then have the group select one. Some that have worked for me include the following:

- work/play
- mother/father
- poor/rich
- old/young
- heaven/hell

4 On the dry-erase board or chart paper make two columns for the contrasting pair and, as a group, brainstorm words and ideas under each. Here's a partial example from a brainstorming session on work/play:

Work	Play
hard	fun
boring	bowling
laid off	relaxing
little pay	TV
bosses	children
good pay	not enough

5 Write the first and seventh lines on the dry-erase board or chart paper and ask volunteers to begin composing the diamante. Continue to highlight the underlying and by now familiar cinquain format and the importance of the pivotal fourth line.

Explore different possibilities for bridging the first three lines with the last three. Here's a group example with two different fourth lines:

> Work
> Long hard
> Tiring boring worrying
> Bosses orders children laughter
> [Little pay much joy]
> Bowling fishing sewing
> Fun friendly
> Play

6 Once students have a grasp of the diamante format, follow the same procedure for the cinquain writing, that is, partner writing, sharing, appreciations, individual writing, and so forth. Circulate and assist where needed. Use the LEA format where necessary.

7 Encourage students to try writing diamantes at home. This is a fun kind of poem for parents to write with children.

KEEPING ELLs IN MIND

1 Cinquains and diamantes are also useful for highlighting parts of speech. *After* students have written poems (remember the focus is on poetry writing!), you can then explore nouns and adjectives and such. Thanh Bui (1999), for example, takes her adult English learners through the process step by step, asking for a single noun to name an object, two adjectives to describe it, and so forth. Moreover, the cinquain readily lends itself to other formats. You can modify it to focus on other parts of speech with your ELLs. Here's an example:

> Laugh (First line, verb)
> Loudly lewdly (Second line, adverbs)
> Danced joked smoked (Third line, three past participles)
> We had a blast (Fourth line, phrase or sentence in the past tense)
> Giggle (Fifth line, another verb)

2 As you write diamantes, it's a good opportunity to work with ELLs on simple opposites and contrasts in English.

WRAP UP

1 This first lesson and introduction to the cinquain format will provide the basis for further cinquain writing; moreover, it will serve as an introduction to the diamante format. The second lesson elaborates and extends the cinquain format and allows students to consider and play around with opposites and contrast.

2 I encourage students to keep a separate folder of all their poetry writing, including cached ideas, drafts in various stages of completion, and final copies. The different kinds of poems they write—lunes, cinquains, diamantes, and so forth—complement one another and often serve as imaginative catalysts for additional poems.

Bio-Poems

Biographical or bio-poems are easy and fun to write. They offer adults another possibility for affirming themselves and expressing who they are, who they might like to become, and what they dream. The power of poetry for many adults with limited literacy abilities is its power of expression, the power to say to the world, "Here I am!" Typically, from my experiences, adults who have not been successful in school had limited opportunities to use writing as a means of asserting their uniqueness and special talents. Bio-poems offer one such opportunity.

There are many different kinds of bio-poems, and I strongly recommend Kenneth Koch's *Wishes, Lies, and Dreams: Teaching Children How to Write Poetry* (1970) for a wealth of possible poetic forms that easily can be modified for adults into elements of bio-poems. Once you and your students begin writing such poems you most likely will begin to collaborate on your own particular formats. The format I suggest in the lesson plan is meant to get you started, but there are many variations.

BEFORE THE LESSON

1 Read through the lesson and decide how long it might take with your particular group of students.

2 Read my example bio-poems and become comfortable with the format. Then write at least two different ones for yourself.

"Frank's Bio-Poem I"

I wish I had more time
To write poems that rhyme
I dreamed I was on stage
And my singing was all the rage
I wanted to run very fast
But I always came in last
I seem to be serious
But I'm often hilarious

"Frank's Bio-Poem II"

I wish I could write prose
Like Papa in his short stories
I dreamed Ernest and I were chasing
Bulls in Spain and fly fishing in Michigan

I wanted to be Hemingway tough
Now trying to write like him is enough
I seem to be an aficionado of Ernest Hemingway
And I really am

The format of this particular bio-poem is as follows:

- I wish

- I dreamed (literally or imaginatively)

- I wanted

- I seem to be/but really am or I seem to be/and am

The poem can be of any length and it might rhyme (as in my first poem) or it might not (as in my second poem). I suggest that you write one that rhymes and one that doesn't. That will give your students options.

3 Make copies of your bio-poems for all students and also prepare a separate sheet of paper that highlights the specific format, that is, I wish, I dreamed, and so on.

THE LESSON

1 Distribute copies of your bio-poems. Tell the students that a bio-poem says something personal about the writer; it gives the reader an insight on the writer's personality. The two bio-poems say something about you and what you wish, dream, and so forth.

2 Read aloud the first bio-poem and have students follow along on their copies. Then read it a second time. Clarify any words or phrases that might be confusing or unknown, for example, *aficionado* and *Hemingway* in my second poem. Ask students for any appreciations and if they learned anything about you that they didn't know before. If they want to read aloud your poems, encourage them to do so. Then read your second poem and follow the same procedure.

3 Distribute the sheets of paper with the highlighted structure of the bio-poem. Ask students to look at your poems and see how they follow the format.

4 Ask students in partner teams, trios, or small groups (depending upon your students, your knowledge of their comfort when interacting with others, and their English language ability) to share things that they wish, dream, want, and seem to be/ but really are. Tell them that they might want to jot down on their sheets of paper any ideas that they like. Circulate among the groups and encourage a wide-ranging discussion and imaginative exploration.

5 After the small groups have discussed ideas ask for volunteers to share briefly. This whole-group sharing and discussion usually generates additional ideas and fosters imaginative "leaps." I have found that often by simply playing around with one part of the bio-poem as a whole class, adults begin to think more figuratively, more imaginatively. Here, for example, are some brainstormed *I seem to be/but really am* ideas from one group of students:

> I seem to be a talker/but I'm really a listener
>
> I seem to be yesterday/but I'm really tomorrow
>
> I seem to be a grape/but I'm really a vine
>
> I seem to be a honeybee/but I'm really a cricket
>
> I seem to be a lake/but I'm really a creek

6 Have students begin their individual bio-poems. Circulate and assist where needed.

7 After students have had an opportunity to work on their first drafts, ask if anyone wants to share a work in progress. Encourage appreciations. Instruct students to continue working on drafts of their bio-poems and, if they are able, to bring in a penultimate draft for sharing at the next class session. At that time final revision and editing can take place with your assistance. Here's a final draft bio-poem by Donovan:

> I wish I could read better
> To get more out of life
> I dream of becoming a chef
> Cooking in a fancy restaurant
> I want to understand
> A lot of words in the dictionary
> I seem to be not religious
> But I want to know God

KEEPING ELLs IN MIND

1 Be sensitive to the fact that adults coming from various parts of the world might at first be hesitant to affirm their individuality. Moreover, some adults might have come from war-torn countries or repressive social contexts and bring with them memories they would rather forget. Bio-poem writing might uncover old wounds. It is of utmost importance that you know your students before you begin something as seemingly simple as a bio-poem.

2 Having students at first dictate all or part of their bio-poems to you or another more skilled student might be necessary for those with very limited English ability.

WRAP UP

1 If you find your students like to write bio-poems, explore with them other possibilities, for example, such stems as *I used to be/but now I am* and *I'm as_____ as a (an)____*. Acrostic or name poems are also viable here, for example:

> **F**riendly
> **R**eader
> **A**ngler
> **N**ightowl
> **K**azemek

2 The more students have opportunities to say something about themselves in various poetic formats the more readily they will take personal, imaginative, and linguistic risks in their writing. Equally important is the way such sharing of oneself with one's peers fosters a sense of group understanding and solidarity.

Apology Poems

I'm sorry. Please forgive me, I didn't mean to do it. Or, perhaps, sorry, I forgot to do it. How many times in our lives have we apologized for something small or large? A thoughtless remark or a failure to follow through on something we promised? How many times have people asked us for forgiveness? If we reflect on our lives, I think we all will be aware of the countless apologies we have given or that have been given to us. Apologizing is an integral part of our lives, and poets through the ages have acknowledged in various ways this act in poems—sacred or secular, serious or lighthearted.

Psalm 51 has David apologizing for sinning with Bathsheba and asking God for forgiveness. It begins,

> Have mercy upon me, O God, according to thy loving kindness: according unto the
>   multitude of thy tender mercies blot out my transgressions.
> Wash me thoroughly from mine iniquity, and cleanse me from my sin.
> For I acknowledge my transgressions: and my sin is ever before me.
> Against thee, thee only, have I sinned, and done this evil in thy sight: that thou
>   mightest be justified when thou speakest, and be clear when thou judgest.

(*The Psalms*, 1997, Psalm 51: 1–4)

William Shakespeare has the speaker in Sonnet 111 asking for pity and forgiveness for the "harmful deeds" he's done:

> O, for my sake do you with fortune chide,
> The guilty goddess of my harmful deeds,
> That did not better for my life provide,
> Than publick means, which publick manner breeds.
> Thence comes it that my name receives a brand,

And almost thence my nature is subdu'd
To what it works in, like the dyer's hand:
Pity me then, and wish I were renew'd;
Whilst, like a willing patient, I will drink
Potions of eysell [vinegar], 'gainst my strong infection;
No bitterness that I will bitter think,
Nor double penance, to correct correction.
Pity me then, dear friend, and I assure ye,
Even that your pity is enough to cure me.

(Shakespeare, 1963, pp. 108–109)

And William Blake reflects on how his act of killing a fly is an occasion for both apology and insight:

"The Fly"

Little Fly
Thy summers play,
My thoughtless hand
Has brush'd away.

Am not I
A fly like thee?
Or art not thou
A man like me?

For I dance
And drink & sing:
Till some blind hand
Shall brush my wing.

If thought is life
And strength & breath:
And the want
Of thought is death;

Then am I
A happy fly,
If I live,
Or if I die.

(Blake, 1988, pp. 23–24)

I have found over the years that writing apology poems with adults and children is an engaging and enjoyable experience for all. This is especially true for adults with different levels of literacy skills and varying levels of English proficiency. This lesson is a simple one that builds on a poem by William Carlos Williams titled "This Is Just to Say" (1986c).

BEFORE THE LESSON

1 Read through the complete lesson and estimate how long it might take with your particular group of students. Decide if any of your ELLs will need additional assistance.

2 Read aloud Williams's poem several times so that you have a sense of its rhythm:

> "This Is Just to Say"
>
> I have eaten
> the plums
> that were in
> the icebox
>
> and which
> you were probably
> saving
> for breakfast
>
> Forgive me
> they were delicious
> so sweet
> and so cold
>
> (Williams, 1986c, p. 372) By William Carlos Williams, from
> *Collected Poems: 1909–1939, Volume I*, copyright 1938 by
> New Directions Publishing Corp. Reprinted by permission
> of New Directions Publishing Corp.

3 Notice the structure of the apology poem:

- What he did ("I have eaten the plums...")
- He asks for forgiveness ("Forgive me...")
- Why he did it ("they were delicious...")

4 Read my apology poem and see how I developed mine around the structure:

> "This Is Just to Say"
>
> I forgot to wash
> my dirty dishes
> after breakfast
>
> I know
> how hard it is
> to scrape
> dried egg yolk

> forgive me
> I was late for class
> and thinking
> of other things

5 Using Williams's poem and mine as examples and the particular structure (that is, what you did, request for forgiveness, and why you did it), write at least two different apology poems. Your poems don't have to deal with any serious lapse on your part; they might be about something as minor as being late to pick up someone, forgetting to send a birthday card, or failing to fill up the auto's gas tank. Try to write one poem that follows pretty closely Williams's poem and then write one in which you vary the format somewhat (as in the cat food example on the next page).

6 Locate examples such as Williams's poem and your own for all students. Also prepare handouts showing the basic format of the apology poem, as noted in step 3.

THE LESSON

1 Share Williams's poem and ask the students to follow along as you read it. Reread the poem several times. (This is also an easy poem for you to memorize.) Ask students if they would like to read along with you on one or two more readings. (You might have to clarify *icebox* for your ELLs and perhaps for younger members of the class.)

2 Ask for responses to the poem. Students will generally comment that "it doesn't sound much like a poem" and "it seems to be a note you'd put on the refrigerator." You might then give them some background on the poem. Williams was a pediatrician who practiced much of his life among the poor and immigrants around Patterson, New Jersey. The story goes that one night he came home late and was hungry. He looked in the icebox, saw a bowl of plums, and ate them. When he got up early the next morning his wife Flossie was still sleeping. He felt guilty about eating the plums, so he wrote her a note which he later shaped into this poem. You might stress to the students that Williams always maintained that poetry could be about *anything*, even eating plums, and that in fact this poem can be seen as a note left on the refrigerator!

3 Distribute copies of your two apology poems. Read them following the procedure described earlier. Ask for appreciations.

4 Distribute the sheets with the basic structure of Williams's apology poem. On the dry-erase board or chart paper make two columns: What You Did and Why You Did It. As a whole class brainstorm some things for which you might want to apologize. Have students jot down on their sheets of paper any of the ideas that they like. Then do the same thing for reasons why these various things might have been done. Tell the students to note on their own papers any of those that they might want to use.

5 Ask the class to select one of the brainstormed ideas, and then as a whole class brainstorm possible ways of shaping it into an apology poem. Here's an example of a class apology poem written about the picking of a flower.

"This Is Just to Say"

I have picked
the last red rose
from our garden
the one which
you smile at
every morning
Forgive me
I wanted it to hold
it was beautiful
and reminded me of you

And here's another one about buying different food for a cat. I especially like this example because it shows how the poem can be played with, that is, only one word on a line and no punctuation.

"My Cat"

Please
forgive
me
for
buying
the
wrong
food
it
was
cheaper
and
I
was
broke

6 After trying out one or two class apology poems, have partners brainstorm any additional ideas they might have for possible topics. (Only do this if particular individuals still are not sure what they might want to write about. Otherwise, let them begin their first drafts.)

7 Have students begin first drafts of their apology poems. Tell them they can follow closely Williams's format (as I did in my dirty dishes example or in one of your own examples) or they can experiment (as in the cat food example). Circulate and assist where needed, perhaps by using an LEA format.

8 Encourage volunteers to share their working drafts. Ask for appreciations from class members. Ask the students to work on their poems before the next class meeting in order to get a draft that they really like. Tell them you'll help them with final editing at that time. Encourage them to write more than one if they'd like.

KEEPING ELLs IN MIND

Apology poems are prime examples of James Britton's (1982) "expressive writing." They allow students to say something about themselves, either serious or humorous. Such expression typically contributes to other creative activities. As Anthony D'Annunzio (1994) discovered in his program for non–English-speaking Cambodians and Hispanics, the LEA activities, individualized reading, and creative writing fostered new opportunities for asserting one's creative potential: "The students easily moved into other expressive activities, such as reading their LEA stories to other classmates, relating experiences, storytelling, skits, and dramatizations—all in English" (p. 161).

WRAP UP

1 Once students have final drafts of their edited apology poems they might want to make greeting cards of them. If you and they have access to computers and one of the many software programs for producing cards, posters, calendars, and so forth, this is a perfect time to make use of it. It's fun, and there is a real audience when, for example, I give my wife a greeting card with my dishes apology poem in it.

2 Tell students that one way of becoming familiar with different types of poetry is to model your own poems on those of other poets. Stress that there's nothing wrong with doing this; they won't be "cheating." Tell them that all writers at one time or another used other writers as their models.

3 The more you incorporate the work of a variety of poets into your class the more your students will be exposed to different ideas, styles, and words. The best way of helping adults to expand their reading and writing vocabularies is to have them actually *use* new words in their own writing. The following lesson, Poems From Poems, will explore this idea in more depth.

Poems From Poems

One interesting and sometimes startling way to write a poem is to use a couple of lines from other poets as a beginning for our own poems. I say "sometimes startling" because we're often surprised at how the lines from a world-renowned poet can inspire us to write poems that we did not know we were capable of. Genius can spark something in us if we're open to it. This is especially true for adult literacy students who finally get the chance to experience some of the best writers and not only the pedestrian writing that they usually find in their workbooks.

Writing poems based on other poets' work encourages us to read more widely in order to become familiar with a variety of poetic voices, formats, and vocabularies that might serve as catalysts for our own writing and that of our students. Similarly, by sharing this variety of poetry with our students—native English speakers as well as those who are learning English as another language—we are helping them to become more skillful in reading and thinking about a range of ideas and forms of discourse. By encouraging them to write in the style of different poets we are helping them to become more facile with their written language, or, as Joseph Brodsky (as cited in Volkov, 1988) contends, giving them "extraordinary speed": "When you compose a single line, things occur to you that in principle shouldn't" (p. 127). Last, by reading widely in poetry and by trying on the styles of different poets, students will soon discover their own favorite poems and poets.

BEFORE THE LESSON

1 Read through the complete lesson and estimate how long it might take with your particular group of students. Decide if any of your ELLs will need additional assistance.

2 Select the opening two lines of poems from some poets that you like and that you think might serve as catalysts for your students' writing. Try to find poems that reflect different styles. If you'd like, as a beginning you might use one or more of my selections. These are poems that I like and have used. Only you know what might be appropriate for your students. Thus, it is necessary for you to read and explore the work of different poets. Following are some examples from Wislawa Szymborska's *View With a Grain of Sand: Selected Poems* (1993):

> My sister doesn't write poems,
> and it's unlikely that she'll suddenly start writing poems.
>
> ("In Praise of My Sister," pp. 112–113)
>
> He came home. Said nothing.
> It was clear, though, that something had gone wrong.
>
> ("Going Home," p. 74)
>
> After every war
> someone has to tidy up.
>
> ("The End and the Beginning," pp. 178–179)

The next set of examples is from *The Complete Poems of Emily Dickinson* (1960):

> "Hope" is the thing with feathers—
> That perches in the soul—
>
> (Poem #254)

Much Madness is divinest Sense—
To a discerning Eye—

(Poem #435)

This is my letter to the World
That never wrote to me—

(Poem #441)

One need not be a Chamber—to be Haunted—
One need not be a House—

(Poem #670)

Two Butterflies went out at Noon—
And waltzed above a Farm—

(Poem #533)

God gave a Loaf to every Bird—
But just a Crumb—to Me—

(Poem #791)

Finally, the last set is from Walt Whitman's *Leaves of Grass* (1983):

Here, take this gift,
I was reserving it for some hero, speaker, or general

("To a Certain Cantatrice," p. 8)

On the beach at night alone,
As the old mother sways her to and fro singing her husky song

("On the Beach at Night Alone," p. 211)

I sit and look out upon all the sorrows of the world, and upon all
    oppression and shame,
I hear secret convulsive sobs from young men at anguish with
    themselves, remorseful after deeds done

("I Sit and Look Out," p. 220)

3 Select two lines from one of the poems you have chosen or from one of those I suggest. Follow the process we have been using, that is, brainstorm, try a first draft, reread it, revise (if you'd like), and complete a final draft that you'll be able to use as an example with your students. I selected Dickinson's "Two Butterflies went out at Noon–And waltzed upon a Farm–" (1960, p. 260). I closed my eyes and tried to see and hear what that might be like if I went out into the forest in summer. Here's my brainstormed list:

Two yellow and black striped butterflies

Floating high above the stream

They almost touch each other at times, but don't

They seem to be looping clockwise

They loop lower and lower until they are only a foot above the stream

They rise then and begin the same dance again

The stream is clear and fast moving

It is only a foot or so deep

It leaps over hunks of granite and fallen branches

It sings as it swirls along

White birches line its banks, their coin-shaped leaves fluttering in the sunshine

Wisps of clouds move quickly overhead

I have elaborated my own brainstorming to highlight the necessity of *you* doing the same. If you are to serve as a model of poetry writing for your students then you must be willing to share the process that you follow.

4 Using your brainstormed list of ideas and images, try a first draft and then as many as you find necessary to complete a model poem for your students. Here's my final draft from Dickinson's lines:

> Two butterflies went out at noon
> And waltzed upon a farm;
> Their steps were yellow, some were black,
> As they gleamed in the sun.
>
> They looped and swirled to the singing
> Stream that bubbled along
> Over well-worn rocks and branches
> Still holding greenery.
>
> Slender birches along the banks
> Joined in the summer's dance,
> Their long limbs swaying in the breeze,
> And leaves gently clapping hands.

5 Now, if you'd like, try the same process with some of the other opening lines. I think you'll get a better sense of the process if you play around with different lines. Here are a couple more of my attempts, one based on Dickinson and one based on Whitman:

> God gave a loaf to every bird,
> But just a crumb to me.

I don't complain, what is the use?
I chew it slowly with my tea.

Here, take this gift,
I was reserving it for some hero, speaker, or general,
But, Mom, I thought that you deserve it more
Than all the men and women living today in our troubled world.
Here is one yellow rose I place on your weathered gravestone:
Spring yellow the color of your gentle soul and common decency
That blossomed and blessed without regard everyone you met.

6 Prepare and use the following for all of your students as examples: the beginning two lines of the various poems, your brainstormed ideas for at least one of your complete poems, any drafts that you might have generated for at least one complete poem, other complete poems that you might have written.

THE LESSON

1 Distribute copies of your poem and have the students follow along as you read it aloud. Read it a second time, and then ask students if they'd like to read it along with you. Ask for appreciations.

2 Describe how you wrote the poem, that is, using the first two lines as a catalyst, brainstorming a list of ideas and images, and so forth. Share any lists and drafts that you might have generated.

3 Read the complete poem from which your first two lines came. Compare it with your poem. Explore how the two poems might be similar or very different. Stress to the students that it's OK to use other writers' lines as inspiration for their own writing (as long as they acknowledge that they've done so). Here's the Dickinson "two butterflies" poem that served as my catalyst:

Two Butterflies went out at Noon—
And waltzed upon a Farm—
Then stepped straight through the Firmament
And rested, on a Beam—

And then—together bore away
Upon a shining Sea—
Though never yet, in any Port—
Their coming, mentioned—be—

If spoken by the distant Bird—
If met in Ether Sea
By Frigate, or by Merchantman—
No notice—was—to me—

(Dickinson, 1960, pp. 260–261)

4 Read aloud the beginning two lines of poems that you've selected and have the students follow along with you. As a group, decide which two lines you'd like to use for a whole-class poem.

5 Write the two lines on the dry-erase board or chart paper and brainstorm possible ideas, words, and images. List them. Once the group has generated a workable list, begin in an LEA manner to compose the poem, that is, read and reread what volunteers contribute, try to get the class to elaborate, modify, move lines around, and so forth. The value of composing a group poem using LEA is that you can show students how they might engage with poetry writing as an exploratory adventure. As an example, here are the two lines of Szymborska's "In Praise of My Sister," a partial brainstormed list, and one of the poems written by a particular group of students:

My sister doesn't write poems,
and it's unlikely that she'll suddenly start writing poems.

(1993, pp. 112–113)

Brainstormed List:

I don't write them either

I do write them

She does start writing them

She does other things

She's a mother

Cooks

Cleans house

Works

Waitress

Writes good letters

Christmas cards

Absent letters for kids

One of the Poems:

My sister doesn't write poems,
And it's unlikely that she'll suddenly start writing poems.
But I've started to write them,
And they're pretty good.
I'll send her one in a Christmas card.

6 After the group has written one or more poems that it likes based upon the first two lines, read the complete poem from which the lines came. Compare the similarities and differences between the poems.

7 Ask individuals, partners, or trios to select two other lines from your list—or lines from another poem or song they might know—and follow the same process described earlier. Circulate and assist where needed. Pair ELLs with native English speakers if necessary.

8 After students have written first drafts have them take the drafts home and continue to play around with them.

KEEPING ELLs IN MIND

1 If you're familiar with poetry in the language of your ELLs, bring in two-line examples in both English and that particular language, for example, here are lines from the Peruvian poet César Vallejo (1978) in Spanish:

Se pedía a grandes voces: They demanded shouting:
—Que muestre las dos manos a la vez.   —Let him show both hands at the same time.

(Nomina de huesos/Payroll of bones, pp. 2–3)

ELLs can then assist their partners (and you!) in composing the poem in both languages.

2 It is possible to modify this lesson for ELLs by selecting only the *first* line of a poem and then asking them to write *only* a second line that completes it in some way. This has the advantage of limiting the amount of writing required for those adults with minimal English ability; however, it also restricts the kind of linguistic exploration, word play, and appreciation for poetic language that come with more expansive writing. Here are some examples completed in an LEA format based on the poetry cited in this lesson.

> My sister doesn't write poems,
> And I don't write them either
>
> God gave a Loaf to every Bird—
> But to some birds more than others
>
> On the beach at night alone,
> I heard the drowned bones singing

WRAP UP

1 This lesson will most likely take several sessions, depending upon your students, the lines selected, and any exploring you might do with poems in two languages. It's best to allow ample time for students to work on their poems during several class meetings. I have found that home responsibilities, work, and so forth often prevent adults from spending much time on a poem at home. However, there are those students who come back to the next session with several poems written. Allow for both types of writers.

2 Final drafts can be collected and included in a class booklet or individuals can create booklets of their own poetry.

3 If there are particular lines and poets that the students especially like, be sure to bring in more of the poetry by that author. Reading more of her or his poetry will help expand the students' reading and writing vocabularies and their love of poetry.

CHAPTER 4

Connecting Music and Literacy

MOST OF US know that music can "soothe the savage breast" and that it often is the "food of love." We all have our favorite kinds of music, whether old Broadway show tunes, classical sonatas, jazz, traditional folk songs, country and western, popular ballads, rock and roll, hip hop, or some other. Many of us listen to music throughout the day, and we know that often it has the ability to lift us if we're feeling blue; moreover, we know it can evoke fond memories of childhood, romance, and cherished moments from the past. As Don Campbell affirms in his well-known book *The Mozart Effect* (1997), music truly is the universal language that can, among various other things, strengthen memory and learning, enhance receptivity to symbolism, and generate a sense of safety and well-being. These are some of the very things we promote in our adult literacy classes.

Psychologists and brain researchers have shown how as infants we are "wired" for a kind of rhythmic understanding and how the brain's activity increases when we actively listen to a piece of music. Music is not only a natural and important part of our heritage as human beings, but it also serves to keep us emotionally and mentally engaged with the world around us and with our pasts. I have found in my writing with adults that music of all kinds can elicit responses; and that particular pieces of music have the ability to call forth images, words, laughter, tears, stories, and poems.

The novelist Lee Smith (1996) once described the work she did with adult literacy students in the mountain region of eastern Kentucky. Florida Slone, a ballad singer, enrolled in the class after she was widowed. She wanted to be able to read her Bible and cookbooks and to write songs and stories. Music was a key component of her literacy development. The program subsequently published Slone's "A Garden of Songs" that included hymns, love ballads, and party tunes (see Smith, 1996). Florida Slone, from my experience, is not unique. Music is often the "hook" that grabs adults' interests and talents. Here, for example, is a poem written by one of my elder students, Dorothea, after she listened to Stephen Foster's "Beautiful Dreamer":

"Dreamer"

Back on the farm,
Relaxing music.
Laying on my back

> Under the trees:
> Watching clouds
> Floating by,
> Wondering what's in
> The great beyond.
> Does it have gold
> And silver streets?

In this chapter we'll extend ideas we've already explored in the chapters on prose vignettes and poetry by connecting those two types of discourse to music. We'll see how music can serve as a catalyst for helping adult students explore their lives and world through writing. Following are three lessons: vignette writing to a favorite piece of music, blues and song writing, and connecting poetry and music.

Vignette Writing to a Favorite Piece of Music

We all have a piece of music that is special to us, that is, some song or melody that immediately makes us recall a happy time or a particular moment when the world was alive with joy and wonder. This lesson is based upon a recalling and retelling of that special moment or time in a prose vignette.

BEFORE THE LESSON

1 Read through the lesson and determine how long it might take with your group of adults. Consider any special adaptations you might have to make for your ELLs. Arrange for any equipment you might need for the lesson, that is, CD player, audiocassette player, or DVD player.

2 Select a piece of music that evokes for you a happy or special time and place. Close your eyes and play the piece of music several times. In your mind's eye and imagination recapture that happy time and place: Where was it? Who was involved? What do you see, feel, hear, smell, and taste? Try to conjure up all of the specifics that the music elicits.

3 After you have immersed yourself in the music try a prose draft capturing all that you experienced while listening. This will serve as a model for your students, so write several drafts until you have one that is good to share. Keep any rough drafts that might also serve as examples for your students. Make copies of your final draft (and any rough drafts if you think they might be helpful) for all students. As an example, here is my music vignette inspired by the Beatles' recording of John Lennon's "In My Life."

> The summer sun rippled through the leaves and sparkled on Cheryl and me as the trio sang "in my life I love you more." We walked from the church out into the garden. The scent of roses mingled with that of the new mown lawn. Gold and pink ribbons draped the trees, and under an old oak Reverend Odom waited for us.

Cheryl smiled at me nervously, and her hazel eyes glistened with excitement. I squeezed her dry hand in my moist and trembling one. I thought as the trio sang "there are places I remember all my life" that I would never forget this place and how her beautiful face shone at this moment.

Our families and friends seated on folding chairs surrounded us with love on that June afternoon so long ago. "Some have gone" as the song continues, "and some remain." At that precious moment in time the world was full of possibilities for us all.

Many years have passed since that summer afternoon. The wedding dress and tuxedo are wrapped in plastic and stored on a back shelf. Our hands bear signs of struggle and age. But, daily, when I look into my wife's hazel eyes, I continue to hear the music, "In my life I love you more."

THE LESSON, PART I

1 Ask students how many have a favorite or special song that is important to them in some way or takes them back to a particular time in their lives. Encourage as many responses as possible. Generally, once a couple of people share, others will remember favorite songs too. Discuss why the songs might be important, when they transport individuals back in time to, specific memories of places that the songs evoke, and so forth. If anyone is willing to sing some or all of his favorite song, encourage him to do so. (I have found that adult students like to sing, and because of church experiences or cultural traditions it is sometimes a creative power among students who struggle most with reading and writing.)

2 Share your favorite song by first playing the CD or audiocassette. (In my example it would be "In My Life," by the Beatles.) Tell students why it is important to you. Read (or sing!) to students the lyrics. Read (or sing) the lyrics a second time, asking the students to join with you. Then play the recording again and ask the students to sing along. If they happen to especially enjoy the song, play it a second time.

3 Distribute copies of your music vignette and read it aloud as the students follow along. Read it a second time, and have them read with you. (In my example, it would be the vignette of my wedding day.)

4 Explain to students how you listened to and used the music to take you back to a particular time and place. Tell them that your music vignette preserves that experience in writing. It is something that can be shared with others.

5 Ask students to think about one or two of their favorite songs before the next class meeting. If they are able to bring in recorded versions of the songs or the printed lyrics, encourage them to do so. Tell them that they'll be capturing their experiences with the music in much the same way that you did with yours.

THE LESSON, PART 2

1 Open the lesson by playing the recording of your favorite song and asking the students to sing along.

2 Ask students in partners or small groups to share the songs they've thought about since the last class meeting. Circulate and encourage sharing. ELLs might bring in songs in their home language. Be sure to highlight and celebrate them. Then as a whole class share what was discussed in the small groups and list the songs on the dry-erase board or chart paper.

3 Ask if anyone has brought in a recorded version of the song. If so, play one or more of the songs. (If everyone has brought in a recording, you most likely will not have the luxury of time to play them all, but try to play at least one in a language other than English if available.)

4 On the dry-erase board or chart paper illustrate how you used the reporter's 5Ws & H to gather and organize the ideas to your experience of a favorite song. Here as an example is my list in an abbreviated manner:

> Who (were you with or who did you share this music with):
> My wife and I; family and friends; etc.
>
> What (images does this music call forth in your mind's eye):
> My wife's smiling face, her wedding dress, my ill-fitting tuxedo, my friend Paul's trio singing for us, etc.
>
> Where (did this music and event occur):
> Palos Heights, Illinois; at a Methodist church
>
> When: June 28, 1970
>
> Why (was the music important then? Why is it still important to you?):
> Then: It was the song we chose for our wedding ceremony
> Now: It captures that moment and day, our youth, and the people there who since have died
>
> How (would you describe this music):
> It's music of love; it evokes my youth and dreams; etc.

5 Discuss with students the value of using such an organizer as the 5Ws & H. Highlight how you used the questions in a flexible manner to generate and organize the ideas and images that came to mind as you listened several times to your particular piece of music.

6 Using your example on the dry-erase board or chart paper as a model, ask the students to jot down the 5Ws & H on one or more pieces of paper. Tell them to leave plenty of space for words, images, and phrases. Depending upon your particular situation, if students brought in recordings and if you have access to multiple audio players, ask students to close their eyes and quietly play their songs. If the students do not have recordings or if multiple players are not available, ask them to close their eyes and hum or sing the songs to themselves. As they listen, hum, or sing, tell them to try to capture all of their feelings that are being stirred by the music.

7 Ask students to jot down words, phrases, and images that came to mind as they experienced their music. Tell them to use the 5Ws & H format, and because they are simply gathering ideas not to worry about spelling or other mechanics. Circulate and assist where needed. Here are some brief excerpts from students' lists:

> Who: myself in church; my husband
> What: "The Little Brown Church in the Vale" by William Pitts—my theme song
> Where: Little Brown Church in Iowa

> ("I Left My Heart in San Francisco" by Tony Bennett)
> When: 1960s in San Francisco
> Why: young then; kind of a hippie
> How: I can still be melted into a weeping ball of emotion

> ("Can't remember the exercise")
> Who: [myself] when I was six or seven
> What: taking piano lessons
> Where: Minneapolis
> How: I couldn't find the middle C without the aid of a keyboard chart; my dreams of being a piano player were shattered

8 Once students have their lists ask them to begin their music vignettes. Stress the importance of trying to write an opening "grabber" sentence or sentences that will make the reader want to read more. Tell them that after they have an opening paragraph they should read it out loud to themselves to hear how it sounds. Then if they'd like they might read it to someone else to learn how it sounds to another person. Circulate and help students if they are having trouble. If necessary use an LEA format with ELLs or those who are experiencing difficulty on beginning their vignettes.

9 Encourage students to continue writing until they get a first draft of their music piece.

10 Before closing the lesson, share with students the drafts that you worked with in order to get your final music vignette. Highlight the various ways you refined your writing. Tell them that as they are thinking about and working on their vignettes before the next class meeting they might want to consider such things as: Does the music vignette have a strong opening? Does it have a memorable closing that will leave the reader with an image in her mind? Are there more particulars (words, images) that will help create a vivid world for the reader? Might lines or phrases from the music be incorporated into the vignette? How does it *sound* as it's read out loud—is there a rhythm and music in the piece?

11 Ask students to bring in all the drafts of their music vignettes for the next class meeting. Once again, encourage them to listen to, hum or sing the songs as they are working with their drafts. Tell them also to bring back or bring for the first time a recorded version of their song.

THE LESSON, PART 3

1   Begin by asking for a volunteer who has a recorded version of his song (with some way to play it for the whole group) and a complete draft of some kind, no matter how rough it is at this point in time. Play the recording and then have the student read the draft. Elicit appreciations from the other class members. Ask the reader to share how he went about getting his ideas, working with them, and then writing this particular draft. What difficulties did he encounter? Follow this process with a second volunteer. What you want to do is to help your students see that writing does *not* simply occur by following a set of steps or a "writing process": prewriting, drafting, revising, editing, and publishing. (Some adults with whom I've worked have had this process drilled into them with little effect other than creating barriers to their writing.) Of course we might follow some general scheme or process when we write, but we are all unique as writers as well as human beings. Idiosyncrasy is important.

2   Ask partners to share their drafts with each other and to offer appreciations. Have them discuss whether or not they are happy with their present drafts. If not, what might they want to do to make them better?

3   Bring the class back together and explore what individuals want or need in relation to their drafts. Typical concerns include such things as making it more lively, being clearer, adding "better" words, making it longer or shorter, fixing up the grammar and other mechanics, and so forth. List these concerns on the dry-erase board or chart paper and address one or two that seem to be common among many students. (In Chapter 7 we will explore some strategies for helping adults to make their writing stronger and related issues of grammar, spelling, and punctuation.)

4   Ask students to continue working on the drafts of their music vignettes. They certainly will be at different stages of completion, and they will have different needs. Circulate and assist individuals as necessary. Encourage all of the students to try to work a bit with their drafts to make them as good as they might be.

5   Have students put away their drafts for further incubation. Return to them if necessary in subsequent meetings and help students shape them into final, edited versions with correct spelling and punctuation. These then might be collected into a class booklet.

KEEPING ELLs IN MIND

1   Adding music into the literacy program for ELLs is certainly one of the most natural and productive things to do. Victoria Purcell-Gates and Robin Waterman (2000), for example, found that the women with whom they were working in a Freirean-

based class not only wanted to be able to read the Bible but also "expressed a desire to be able to read the songbooks that are used in these religious services" (p. 83).

2 When students sing or share songs in their home or second language, Stephen Krashen's (1982) "affective filter" is lowered. The input of the music is interesting and pleasurable; moreover, it usually is easy to understand because of rhyme, repetition, relative brevity, and predictability. (See, for example, Marcia Farr's 1994 description of how a group of "Chicago Mexicanos" use songs and song lyrics to celebrate a Christmas season religious event.)

3 In addition to writing brief vignettes about favorite songs, ELLs can also listen at home to favorite songs in English. Repeated listening helps them tune into the flow and rhythm of the language. The lyrics of favorites then can be transcribed, and adults can use the lyrics in conjunction with the recorded music for further writing and reading.

WRAP UP

We and our students live in a world of multiple literacies. Indeed, for those adults who lack the kinds of reading and writing skills that will enable them to pursue their particular personal, social, and economic goals, oral and visual media are often the primary means of connecting to the wider world. Because they might listen to or sing and play music of different kinds for different purposes, most adult literacy students (and ourselves as their teachers) are able to make immediate connections with music of some sort. We all have our favorites, and our favorites can help us engage in the reading and writing of texts. This is true no matter if our students are native English speakers from an urban background or ELLs from rural and underdeveloped parts of the world. Music vignettes help adults ground their writing and reading in musical experiences that are resonant in their lives.

Blues and Song Writing

People have been singing the blues forever it seems. They sing when they are sad, lonely, hungry, depressed, or miserable after someone they love leaves them. Woody Guthrie, America's great folk balladeer, wrote that a "flat blue million songs have already been written and sung about the fight you've got to put up to keep your mouths half fed and your house and home going" (1965, p. 75). He then proceeded to list 150 possible blues titles. Here are 10 of them: "No Money Blues," "No Job Blues," "Hungry Heart Blues," "Mortgage Day Blues," "Low Pay Work Hand," "Inflation Struggle," "Hungry Baby Blues," "Gone Woman Blues," "Gone Man Blues," and "Headache for Breakfast" (pp. 75–77). The unique thing about the blues is that simply by singing them people feel better. Although they typically are about sad or depressing topics, blues are really an affirmation of life, and as Don Campbell (1997) observes, they can "uplift and inspire, release deep joy and sadness, convey wit and irony, and affirm our common humanity" (p. 79).

The African American poet Quincy Troupe observed that the blues is a distinct language:

> The blues is constructed close to the way Americans, and especially African Americans from the Midwest and the South, speak. We tend to speak in circles—we come back and say things over and over again, just for emphasis—and there you have the whole repetition of lines coming back like refrains. (as cited in Moyers, 1995, p. 417)

It is the voice of vernacular language, repetition, and topics we all can relate to that make the blues so vital in an adult literacy class. The blues are fun to sing, the lyrics are easy to read and interesting to write, and recordings are readily available.

BEFORE THE LESSON

1. Read through the lesson and determine how long it might take with your group of adults. Consider any special adaptations you might have to make for your ELLs. Arrange for any equipment you might need for the lesson, that is, CD player, audiocassette player, or DVD player.

2. Select a simple blues recording that you like, one that might serve as a viable example for your students. Play it several times in order to be sure that the singer's words are understandable. (It is sometimes difficult to determine all of the words of a blues song. You want a clear model, at least for the first attempt.) Ensure that your selection follows the blues pattern: the first two lines are repeated as a declaration of some sort; then a new statement is made that is a response to them or completes the stanza with a twist or the way a punch line might complete a joke. There are variations on this form of course, but the use of repetition and rhyme is essential. Here are two examples of classic blues. The first is "Gulf Coast Blues" by Clarence Williams (1923):

> "Gulf Coast Blues"
>
> The man I love he has done left this town,
> The man I love he has done left this town.
> And if it keeps on snowing I will be Gulf Coast bound.
>
> The mailman passed but he didn't leave no news.
> The mailman passed but he didn't leave no news.
> I'll tell the world he left me with those Gulf Coast blues.
>
> Some of you men sure do make me tired.
> Some of you men sure do make me tired.
> You've got a mouth full of "gimme," a handful of "much oblige."

The second example is "The Broadway Blues" by J. Brandon Walsh and Terry Sherman (1915), originally introduced in the vaudeville era by Sophie Tucker.

Oh there's no use talking folks I'm feeling blue,
Oh there's no use talking folks I'm feeling blue
All alone in New York town and loaded down
with the mean old blues
Those Broadway blues.

Got to go and get myself some gin right now
Got to go and get myself some gin right now
It's an awful thing when gloom keep hanging 'round
With the Broadway blues, those Broadway Blues.

CHORUS
Oh the blues, oh the blues,
did you ever have the Broadway blues,
They're the meanest old Blues,
those nasty Broadway Blues.

"Gulf Coast Blues" is available on Bessie Smith's *Greatest Hits* (2005) CD. You also can check with your local record store, online retailer, or on iTunes.

THE LESSON, PART I

1 Ask your students how many have ever listened to the blues. Do they have any favorite blues singers? Have they ever had the blues? Share a time when you did. (We all have had the blues, and this generally leads to a wide-ranging discussion.)

2 Introduce the blues song that you have selected. Tell the students simply to sit back and listen. Play the song a second time. Ask the students what they think of it. Does it connect with any of their experiences?

3 Play the blues a third time, asking the students to sing along.

4 Explore the basic structure of the blues by reading and highlighting the use of line and word repetition and rhyme.

5 Brainstorm and list possible topics for a blues song. As a whole class select one of the topics and compose in an LEA style the first stanzas of two or three different blues songs. As an example, here are the first stanzas from different blues lyrics, written using an LEA format, on the topic of work:

I worked at the car wash for one month
I worked at the car wash for one month
But the hours aren't the greatest
And the money ain't enough

We were working up on street level
Yeah, we were working up on street level
The crane pulley dropped where we were standing
We could've all been killed

> I was working at the prison
> I was working at the prison
> There's a lot of crazy people there
> There's a lot of crazy people there

6 Have partners discuss possible blues topics they might like to think about and possibly write about as individuals before the next class meeting. Circulate and assist where needed. You might have to clarify and elaborate for your ELLs. Ask students to jot down one or two topics for their blues composition. (I constantly stress the importance of using writing as a means of caching ideas and as a memory aid.) Before ending the session, ask everyone to share one of the possible topics. Tell them if they'd like they might try to write at home a draft of at least the first stanza of their blues song. If any of them have favorite blues recordings at home, ask them to bring them to the next meeting.

THE LESSON, PART 2

1 Before the next class meeting write your own blues song and make copies for all students. Here's mine as an example:

> "Growing Old Blues"
>
> Woke up this morning creaky knees and back
> Woke up this morning creaky knees and back
> I wish this growin' old would give me some slack
>
> Went for a little walk on the ice and snow
> Yeah, went for a little walk on the ice and snow
> Slippin' like a geezer and slidin' so slow
>
> Ate my bowl of oatmeal sugar and cream
> Ate my bowl of oatmeal sugar and cream
> Three eggs and bacon just a faded dream
>
> Ten o'clock in the morning ready for a nap
> Ten o'clock in the morning ready for a nap
> I wonder what happened to all my youthful sap

2 If any students have brought in CDs or audiocassettes of favorite blues selections, play one or more. (Be sure to bring in a couple of new examples just in case your students don't have any to share.) Highlight again the format of the blues and the importance of word and line repetition and rhyme. (We'll discuss in a later chapter the importance of meaningful repetition for adult literacy students.)

3 Distribute copies of the blues you wrote. Read (or better yet, sing) it aloud while the students follow along. Ask them for any appreciations.

4 Ask for volunteers to share what they've thought about or written since the last class meeting. (Sometimes because of their busy lives students will not have written much. This is an appropriate time to stress once again the value of writing—however briefly—in a journal on a daily basis.) Encourage appreciations.

5 Ask students to continue or begin to work on their blues as individuals or with partners. If they have a first draft, ask them to look at it again with the intent of producing a final draft. Assist where needed in terms of helping ELLs with vocabulary and grammar and native English speakers with spelling, and so forth.

6 As a conclusion to the session, ask for a volunteer with a fairly complete draft to share it. As a whole group, help the writer decide on a particular way to sing the first stanza.

7 Encourage students to complete their blues song by the next class meeting.

THE LESSON, PART 3

1 Begin the session by having partners or small groups share the drafts of their blues songs. Try to get a fairly finished draft from all students (although the spelling and punctuation might not be perfect). Focus most of your attention at the beginning of the lesson on your ELLs, helping them complete their blues composition.

2 Devote the rest of the session (or at least a substantial portion of it depending upon your time frame) to a sharing and singing of the students' blues. Encourage appreciations. Here as an example is a blues song by Glen:

"Weary, Weary Morning"

Oh, weary, weary morning
Oh, weary, weary morning
I wake up in the morning
With my mind all tied up in knots.

Go to work and do my job
Go to work and do my job
Start a new day over again
The same thing all over again.

So my weary, weary bones
So my weary, weary bones
Are so tired and alone
Won't somebody help me please

3 Collect the students' blues songs at the end of the session.

KEEPING ELLs IN MIND

1 Because of the rhyme, rhythm, repetition, and emotional content of most blues compositions, they will connect with all adults, including ELLs. The limited vocabulary allows for meaningful repetition and practice, for example, Glen's *Go to work and do my job*.

2 An LEA format can be followed with individual ELLs or with a small group (if you have several in your class). As a scribe you can help shape into English the individual's or group's ideas. A single stanza is enough.

3 The differences between written and spoken vernacular English can be highlighted with many blues songs, for example, *'cause* (*because*) and my *slippin'* (*slipping*).

4 You can record the class singing its blues collection and then make multiple copies of the CD or audiocassette. In this manner students at home will be able to listen to the music as they follow along in the songbook. (See Wrap Up for instructions.) This will be especially beneficial for your ELLs.

WRAP UP

1 Collect the students' blues into a class songbook with a title such as "Our Blues." These can then be sung at various times, for example, before or at the end of a particular class meeting.

2 I have used the blues as the basis for this song writing lesson because feeling blue is something we all can relate to and because of the repetitious and rhymed nature of blues lyrics. The structure of this lesson can be followed for just about any other type of music. Depending upon the students in your class, you might want to use rap, country, rock and roll, folk, or pop music as the basis. Almost all of these make use of repetition, rhyme, and rhythm in some fashion. The important thing is to connect the writing to the kinds of music students listen to or sing outside of class.

Poetry and Music

I have written elsewhere "[music] and poetry just naturally seem to go together. Many kinds of music can stir in our imaginations vivid pictures of different settings, people, and things" (Kazemek, 2002a, p. 195). Over the years I have found this to be true while writing with adult literacy students, elders, elementary and secondary school students, and university students preparing to become teachers. And in my experience this also has been true while working with native English speakers in the United States and Canada, or with English as a Foreign Language students in Norway, Lithuania, Ghana, and Ukraine. The poet Kenneth Koch (1977) observed, "Writing 'to music' can be a little bit like writing to secret excited feelings, the music being like a physical form of inspiration" (p. 107). Indeed, music serves as a natural metaphor maker and poetry producer.

In his ethnographic study of literacy in the lives of people in a Newfoundland fishing community, "Bridget's Harbour," William Fagan (1998) found,

> One form of oral language that is alive and well in the Bridget's Harbour area is the composition and rendition of song. The number of local songs named ranged from twenty to thirty-eight per interviewed group, and the number of local singers named ranged from thirteen to twenty-one per group. Song was not just a means for socializing; it presented an avenue for expression. Through song, the people found occasions to laugh, to cry, to raise issues, and even sometimes to suggest solutions. (pp. 120–121)

Unfortunately, many adult students who struggle with reading and writing have seldom experienced opportunities to write about secret excited feelings or to use song as an avenue for expression. They were marched or drilled through workbooks and, more recently, computer programs that packaged literacy as a commodity, one that is valued by test scores, levels of comprehension, and so forth. As Barry Sanders (1994) maintains,

> Reading and writing are being lost as activities that transform a person into an entirely different creature, a person who has the capability of making continual discoveries about himself or herself. They are being lost as activities through which one finds constant surprises in sentences—both written *and* spoken—and in the self. (p. 200)

Connecting poetry writing and reading to music fosters continual discoveries and constant surprises among adults. Such connections help adults experience the wonder, mystery, and potential power of literacy and music. As Bob Dylan (2004) observes, "A song is like a dream, and you try to make it come true. They're like strange countries that you have to enter" (p. 165). Writing is no longer little more than some set of skills, rules, and grammar, and music is not something simply to listen to. Instead, both are forces for personal and social transformation that invite us to a lifelong journey of discovery. The great tenor saxophonist John Coltrane said it best with regard to music:

> I want to discover a method so that if I want it to rain, it will start immediately to rain. If one of my friends is ill, I'd like to play a certain song and he'll be cured. When he'd be broke, I'd bring out a different song, and immediately he'd get all the money he needed. But what these pieces are, and what is the road to attain the knowledge of them, that I don't know. The true powers of music are still unknown. To be able to control them must be, I believe, the goal of every musician. (as cited in Kahn, 2002, pp. 192–193)

Substitute *literacy* for *music* in the penultimate sentence and *reader and writer* for *musician* in the last sentence and you'll understand better the purpose of this lesson and, indeed, this whole book.

BEFORE THE LESSON

1 Read through the lesson and determine how long it might take with your group of adults. Consider any special adaptations you might have to make for your ELLs. Arrange for any equipment you might need for the lesson, that is, a CD player or audio-cassette player.

2 Select one or more pieces of instrumental music, for example, classical, jazz, pop, new age, and so forth. Pick some music that you like, but don't be afraid to expand and experiment with music you don't typically listen to. (At the end of this lesson I list some composers and performers that I like and have found to be accessible to adolescents and adults of all ages.)

3 Relax and listen to one piece of music with your eyes closed. Listen to it a couple of times. While listening, think about the following:

- What do you see?
- Where are you?
- How do you feel?
- Do you smell anything?
- What might you taste?
- Do you hear anything?

4 Now jot down the images that you saw in your mind's eye while listening. As an example, here's a list I made after listening to "Spring" from Vivaldi's "Four Seasons":

> north woods of Minnesota
> pines
> in April wind
> young trees leaning on the old
> long needles
> a red cardinal singing
> scraps of pine cones on the ground
> somewhere above squirrels chatter
> scent of decaying needles on the ground
> I feel excited about the rebirth of the earth
> distant lapping of waves on lake shore

5 Once you have a list of images, feelings, smells, and so forth, arrange some of them into a short poem that might or might not rhyme. Here are two examples from my list:

> Amongst the long-needled pine
> A cardinal sings of spring
> Squirrels chatter winter stories
> Lying in scraps on the ground

In the North Woods
I walk upon old pinecones
Decaying needles
And am happy alone.

6 Here's another example by Nette after she listened to one of Miles Davis's ballads:

The cat is sleeping
The candlelight burns out
Dark
Quiet
No laugh
No cry
No smile
Dark
Alone
Tunes from a trumpet
It's quiet
Dark

7 You might want to follow the same process with a second piece of music in order to have a couple of examples for your students. Make copies for your students of your list(s) and the poem(s) that you created after listening to the music.

THE LESSON, PART I

1 Explain what you have in mind for the lesson. Play the piece of music that you responded to by listing and writing a poem. Ask the students to close their eyes and just listen.

2 Ask the students what they felt or pictured while they were listening. Elicit as many responses as possible. Explain to them that music, especially instrumental music of various kinds, can call to mind many memories and even help us create new images, events, and stories.

3 Share what you previously did as you listened and then how you brainstormed a list of words and images that you shaped into a poem. Distribute your list and poem as examples. Read your poem a couple of times.

4 Write on the dry-erase board or chart paper the following questions that helped you attend more closely to the music:

What do you see?
Where are you?
How do you feel?
Do you smell anything?
What might you taste?
Do you hear anything?

5 Ask the students to attend to those questions with closed eyes as you play a new piece. Tell them to relax and let themselves be taken into the music. (I almost always use a jazz ballad by John Coltrane, Keith Jarrett, Branford Marsalis, Miles Davis, Sonny Rollins, or others for this first activity. A meditative piece of music usually calls forth a rich variety of images, memories, and responses.)

6 Ask partners to share what they saw, felt, smelled, and so forth, and then have the class as a whole share. (If necessary, play the piece of music a second time.) List their responses on the dry-erase board or chart paper. Here's a partial list from a group of students after listening to one of John Coltrane's ballads, "Say It (Over and Over Again)."

waiting

waves breaking

loss

ocean

saxophone crying

woman on shore

sailor gone to sea

no stars

widow

7 Once you have exhausted the ideas, ask the class to shape some of the words and phrases into a poem that complements the music. Practice an LEA format as the students dictate and you write, read, and repeat what they have offered. Here's a draft of the poem the students created from the Coltrane list.

As the saxophone plays
Waiting
Longing
Wailing on shore
The ocean took him
Far away
The waves breaking
On shore won't
Bring him back
Widow wailing
Longing
Waiting
As the saxophone plays

8 Read and reread the poem several times, and then ask the students to read it with you. If they like they might copy the poem in their journals or writing notebooks. (See my comments in Keeping ELLs in Mind further in this section.)

9 Ask the students to try to listen to one or more pieces of instrumental music they might have at home or that they might hear on the radio. (If you have a classical or jazz radio station in your community, you can give them the frequency of the station.) Tell them to listen to the music and let themselves be carried away with it or into it. They might individually follow the same process at home if they like, that is, listening, listing, and drafting a poem. If they have favorite selections they'd like to share with the whole group, ask them to bring the music to the next class session. (If you have a personal collection of CDs or other audio recordings that you'd be willing to lend, do so. I find it a good way to introduce people to new music. Of course if some of your students have MP3 players and download music from sources such as iTunes, you can suggest that they download certain pieces of music.)

THE LESSON, PART 2

1 Open the session by playing a new piece of music. If you used jazz the previous session, use a classical piece this time. (For example, I usually follow up with Debussy's "La Mer.") Ask students to close their eyes and simply listen in order to get everyone back into the spirit of music and poetic language. Briefly share responses.

2 Ask if anyone listened and wrote something at home since the last class meeting. If anyone has, ask her to share the music and what she wrote.

3 If students brought in new pieces of music to play, select one of them for the rest of the lesson. If no one has brought in anything new (and this happens), then select one of the pieces from among your recordings.

4 Follow the same format used in Part 1 of the lesson, that is, listen and have partners share, discuss, and list. Only this time ask individuals to try and draft their own poems, or, particularly with ELLs and those least proficient native English speakers, have partners compose a poem together. Circulate and assist as needed. Play the music in the background while students are composing.

5 Once students have rough drafts ask for volunteers to share. Encourage appreciations.

6 Students subsequently can work on their drafts until they have versions they like. These then can be collected into a class booklet or kept in individual folders.

KEEPING ELLs IN MIND

Daniel Alderson (1996) suggests copying poems by hand in a notebook or journal. Such copying is especially valuable for ELLs.

> This process allows you to internalize the poem, to drink it in in its most minute detail in a way that reading never does... Although it may be boring and you might be tempted to skip it, copying by hand is extremely important because it makes you notice it. (p. 13)

Indeed, as Francine Filipek Collignon (1994) found in her literacy work with Hmong women, "Practices—such as dictation or copying—are not distasteful to people who have integrated them as part of well-developed functional systems for learning [such as stitching 'paj ntaub' embroidery]" (p. 340).

WRAP UP

1   I have written elsewhere that music "gives us a space, some objective distance, within which to reflect on our lives, loves, pasts, presents, and possible futures" (Kazemek & Rigg, 1997, p. 141). Once you begin to use different kinds of instrumental music for poetry writing and as background to other class activities, I'm sure you will see its power. Moreover, you and your students will find it enjoyable as well and be eager to explore different types of music for pleasure and as catalysts for writing.

2   Following is a list of some performers and composers that I have found to be effective with different students at different times. This list is idiosyncratic, and my choices might or might not resonate with you or your students. I offer it as a place to start. The best list is the one you and your students develop together.

Jazz

John Coltrane: "Ballads," "The Gentle Side of John Coltrane"

Miles Davis: "Kind of Blue," "Sketches of Spain"

Bill Evans: "Waltz for Debby"

Keith Jarrett: "Köln Concert," "Paris Concert"

Thelonious Monk: "Straight No Chaser"

Classical

Beethoven: "Moonlight Sonata," "6th Symphony (Pastoral)"

Claude Debussy: "Clair de lune," La mer"

Philip Glass: "Glassworks"

Igor Stravinsky: "The Rite of Spring"

Tan Dun: "Crouching Tiger, Hidden Dragon"

CHAPTER 5

Connecting Art and Literacy

I HAVE DISCUSSED the value of metaphorically considering adult literacy as story-telling, that is, seeing print literacy as one way of exploring, expressing, and sharing our lives, our stories, with other people (Kazemek, 1991). Other forms of meaning making, however, especially visual and musical art, also allow us to engage in such storytelling. Thus, two relevant questions arise: "How can visual and musical art deepen and broaden our understanding of literacy?" and "How can literacy deepen and broaden our understanding of those arts?" (Kazemek & Rigg, 1997, p. 137). We explored in the last chapter ways of using music in the adult literacy program. In this chapter we'll look at the role that visual art—both the "serious" and the "everyday"—might play in foster-ing purposeful writing among adult students.

Art in adult literacy education is even more important today than when I wrote those words in 1997. Since that time the dismal reductionism that is the hallmark of much literacy education in schools has found its way into the adult classroom. Eric Weiner (2005/2006) observes,

> The Partnership for Reading (PFR) in the United States has recently thrown its hat into the ring of adult literacy research and practice.... PFR advocates for a narrow, school-based conception of reading, excluding from its recommendations several aspects of literacy development that have been determined by many adult educators, scholars, and practitioners to be vital for the successful development of competent readers and writers. (p. 286)

And George Demetrion (2005) maintains that "there is little present inclination to em-brace the U.S. democratic and constitutional ethos to situate the politics of adult lit-eracy in the construction of a federal or national vision" (p. 293).

Why art at all one might ask? John Dewey answers that question in *Art as Experience* (1934): "The expressions that constitute art are communication in its pure and undefiled form. Art breaks through barriers that divide human beings, which are impermeable in ordinary associations" (p. 244). Visual art, like music, allows us and our students to connect and communicate in ways that are sometimes blocked because of language differences, restricted skills, and divergent experiences. Whether examin-ing, appreciating, and discussing a Hmong "paj ntaub" or story cloth, the copperplate engraving of an Inuit artist, a somber painting by Edward Hopper, a Depression-era photograph by Walker Evans, or a picture of a Mexican mural, we and our students intuitively know that we are in the presence of something that expresses our common humanity.

In her annotated bibliography of books for adult new readers, Marguerite Crowley Weibel (1996) says that "art and photography provide a good starting point for writing exercises because they provide information and ideas that students can describe, compare, react to, or connect to their own experiences and ideas" (p. 2). Moreover, she highlights the fact that most public libraries have varied collections of useful art books and books of photography. In this chapter we'll explore in four lessons ways of connecting writing to visual works of art: Writing About Paintings (or Other Works of Art), Writing About Other People's Photographs, Writing About Our Own Photographs, and Writing About Art in Everyday Life.

Writing About Paintings (or Other Works of Art)

Collaborations between visual and literary artists offer adult literacy students wonderful examples of how one work of art, say, a painting, can inspire another, say, a poem. There are several fine collections of such pairings, and they are readily accessible at local libraries or from booksellers. Kenneth Koch and Kate Farrell's beautiful collection *Talking to the Sun: An Illustrated Anthology of Poems for Young People* (1985) is certainly my favorite and that of many teachers at all levels. Although it is subtitled "for young people," it is a collection for anyone who appreciates art and poetry. Koch and Farrell chose paintings and other works of art from the Metropolitan Museum of Art's extensive exhibits to illustrate poems from many different traditions and in many different forms. Moreover, Kate Farrell has subsequently compiled *Art and Love: An Illustrated Anthology of Love Poetry* (1990) that pairs more poems with works from the Metropolitan Museum and *Time's River: The Voyage of Life in Art and Poetry* (1999) that marries artworks from the U.S. National Gallery of Art with poems.

While pairings of poetry and art from such collections make wonderful catalysts for students' writing, in this lesson I want to use as examples poems by William Carlos Williams, a painting by the 16th-century Flemish master Pieter Brueghel the Elder, and a painting by the 20th-century American painter Charles Demuth. Together they model for students how a work of art can inspire a creative piece of writing, and likewise how a poem can inspire a work of art.

BEFORE THE LESSON

1   Read the 10 poems that Williams (1988c, pp. 385–394) wrote based on different paintings by Brueghel, for example, "Hunters in the Snow," "Peasant Wedding," and "Children's Games." For this lesson I'm using "The Corn Harvest":

Summer!
the painting is organized
about a young

reaper enjoying his
noonday rest
completely

relaxed
from his morning labors
sprawled

in fact sleeping
unbuttoned
on his back

the women
have brought him his lunch
perhaps

a spot of wine
they gather gossiping
under a tree

whose shade
carelessly
he does not share the

resting
center of
their workaday world

2 Locate a copy of Brueghel's painting (it's titled *The Harvesters* and not "The Corn Harvest" as in Williams's poem) in a collection from your local library or from one of various sites on the Internet (see Figure 1). Explore it closely and notice the manner in which Williams's poem simply describes what he sees in the painting.

3 Locate and read a poem about a painting or other work of art such as Williams's "The Great Figure":

Among the rain
and lights
I saw the figure 5
in gold
on a red
firetruck
moving

Figure 1. *The Harvesters*, **Pieter Brueghel**

The Metropolitan Museum of Art, Rogers Fund, 1919 (19.164). Image © The Metropolitan Museum of Art

tense
unheeded
to gong clangs
siren howls
and wheels rumbling
through the dark city.

(Williams, 1986a, p. 174) By William Carlos
Williams, from *Collected Poems: 1909–1939*,
Volume I, copyright 1938 by New Directions
Publishing Corp. Reprinted by permission of
New Directions Publishing Corp.

4   Then find a copy of Charles Demuth's painting *The Figure 5 in Gold* in either a library collection or from one of the Internet sites (see Figure 2; Williams's poem and Demuth's painting can also be found in Kenneth Koch and Kate Farrell's *Talking to the Sun*, 1985, p. 130). Demuth was a friend of Williams, and the poem inspired him to

Figure 2. *The Figure 5 in Gold*, **Charles Demuth**

The Metropolitan Museum of Art, Alfred Stieglitz Collection, 1949 (49.59.1). Image © The Metropolitan Museum of Art

make this painting. Notice how he captures the front of the fire truck with the three 5s, and how he includes "Bill" and "WCW" on the engine. The painting is alive with energy and is a perfect complement to the poem.

THE LESSON, PART I

1 Share Brueghel's painting with your students. Briefly provide some background on the artist. Ask students to look at the painting carefully, focusing on all of the specific things they might see in it. Tell them nothing is too small or insignificant. (If you're able to make a colored overhead transparency of the painting, have access to a document camera, or can project from your computer, all the better. That will help students explore the painting more closely.)

2 After students have had time to appreciate the painting, ask for volunteers to share various things that they notice. Make a list on the dry-erase board or chart paper. You will typically get responses like wheat fields, stacks, bread, bowl of soup, houses, scythe, basket, roads, church steeple, and so forth.

3 Tell students that looking at a painting or photograph closely and carefully is similar to good writing: the more detailed and concrete the writing the better. (You might even cite William Carlos Williams's admonition: "no ideas but in things" [1963, p. 6].)

4 Share with students Williams's poem, "The Corn Harvest." Tell students that Williams loved the paintings of Brueghel and wrote poems about 10 of them. Ask the students to follow along as you read the poem. Read it a second time, and then ask the class to read along with you. Ask for volunteers to share what they think of the poem and the way in which it complements the painting. Students typically will comment that the poet is simply describing what he sees. You also will get responses that highlight the fact that the poem focuses on one part of the painting (the sleeping man and gossiping women) and the way the poem takes you imaginatively into the scene ("perhaps/a spot of wine").

5 Using an LEA format, encourage the whole class to try writing a little poem about the painting. Use the list of things they saw as a beginning. While scribing the students' suggestions you might write them in a manner similar to Williams's poem, that is, short lines and three-line stanzas. Here are a couple of poems students have generated in the past:

> Three men working
> Hauling
> Cutting and winnowing.
>
> The owner
> In the big house
> Is watching
> From the window
> Wondering when
> They'll get back to work.

6 Share with students Williams's poem "The Great Figure." Read it twice and then ask the students to read along with you. Explain any words that might cause difficulty for your ELLs, for example, *unheeded*. After asking students what they think of the poem, be sure to highlight the fact that it was based on a simple experience, that of watching a fire truck race by on its way to a fire. (I hate to belabor it, but the more you can get adult literacy students to see that poetry and other kinds of writing need not be mysterious the better.)

7 Now share with students Demuth's painting, *The Figure 5 in Gold*. Explain how in the first painting and poem the painting came first, that is, Williams studied the painting and then wrote a poem about it. In this second case the poem came first.

Demuth, a painter friend of Williams, liked the poem and then captured it in his work of art. Be sure to point out the particulars in the painting if students don't notice them (but they almost always do), that is, C.D., WCW, Carlos, and so forth.

8 Conclude the lesson by asking students to try to write their own poem about Demuth's painting for the next class. Tell them it doesn't have to be long and they should follow the same process they did with the Brueghel painting.

THE LESSON, PART 2

1 Begin the lesson by again reading "The Great Figure" while showing the painting (on a colored overhead transparency, document camera if you have one, or directly from the Internet if you happened to have the appropriate technology). Ask for volunteers who might like to read the poem a second or third time.

2 Ask if anyone had a chance to write a poem about the painting. Sometimes, for various reasons, no one will have written one. Be sure that you have your own example to share. Here's an example composed by a student; the second example is one I wrote:

> 555
> clang clang clang
> watch out!
> someone's house is burning!
>
> The fire engine
> Red and gold
> With grim-faced men
> Wondering how much
> Soot they will have to swallow

3 Distribute a varied selection of artwork complemented by poetry that represents different countries, ethnic groups, cultures, styles, and so forth. You can gather these from your local library by using Marguerite Crowley Weibel's (1996) annotated bibliography as a guide, locating the several collections by Kenneth Koch and Kate Farrell that I discussed at the beginning of this chapter, and talking with your local librarian. (For example, Farrell's 1999 collection includes such imaginative pairings as a Lucille Clifton poem with a Cézanne painting and Langston Hughes with van Gogh.)

"i live in music" (1999) is a single poem by the African American poet Ntozake Shange that links together stunning paintings of blues and jazz musicians by the late Romare Bearden. This book has been a favorite because students like Bearden's expressive collages and Shange's use of rich poetic imagery, vernacular language, and nonstandard spelling: "i got 15 trumpets where other women got hips"; "hot like peppers i rub on my lips/thinkin they waz lilies"; "hold yrself in a music." (Of course, you'll have to explain and clarify this usage for your ELLs.)

A book series that I especially like is Art & Poetry, which includes wonderful pairings of famous artists and poets/song writers. The series includes *Shape of My Heart* (1998) with a poem by the rock musician Sting and abstract paintings by Pablo Picasso, *Over the Rainbow* (2000) with lyrics from the movie by E.Y. Harburg and paintings by Maxfield Parrish, and *May I Feel Said He* (1995) with poems by e.e. cummings and paintings by Marc Chagall. The most recent addition to the series is *Dance Me to the End of Love* (2006), a lovely, richly romantic pairing of the song by Leonard Cohen and paintings by Henri Matisse.

As with any text or work of art that you use with adult students you have to be sensitive to different religious, cultural, and moral sensibilities. Some of cummings's witty, sexy poems might offend some individuals.

4 Encourage students to work as partners. Pair your ELLs with more capable native English speakers. Ask them to browse through the collections, appreciate the art, and read any of the poems that grab them. Encourage partners to read the poems aloud together. Circulate and offer assistance where needed in terms of possible explanations, vocabulary, and so on. Allow plenty of time for appreciation. Many adult literacy students have never had the opportunity to enjoy art in the basic skills classes.

5 After partners have browsed through the artwork and read one or more of the poems, ask them to select one of the pieces of art and together write a short poem that complements it. Have them follow the same close study, listing, and drafting process they followed with the two poems by Williams and the accompanying paintings by Brueghel and Demuth. Circulate and help where needed. Use an LEA strategy with ELLs and those least proficient native English speakers if necessary.

6 Before the closing of the lesson ask for volunteers to share any drafts that they have written. Encourage appreciations from the rest of the class. Here's an example from two students who used a page from *Over the Rainbow*. Two paintings by Maxfield Parrish were featured with the words, "Somewhere over the rainbow skies are blue." The students wrote the following:

> In the world these days
> It seems there is not that much love.
> All the teenagers, the homeless.
> They ain't getting that much love.

7 Encourage partners and individuals to continue using the collections to explore different kinds of art and complementary poetry. Ask them to try writing their own poems for paintings that capture their imaginations.

KEEPING ELLs IN MIND

LEA composition about works of art as a whole class and with a native–English speaking partner provides for modeling of spoken and written English and supports ELLs' efforts. Kathleen Mohr (1999) observes,

LEA values the experiential and language backgrounds of the students and enables each student to participate from his or her own point on the continuum of language skills. Its emphasis on shared oral language that is used as a basis for reading and writing provides a strong platform for launching successful literacy development for ESL students of any age. (p. 238)

WRAP UP

Using works of art as catalysts for writing can—and I maintain should—be an ongoing activity. There is always at least a small amount of time each class session for the viewing and sharing of lovely things. In addition to using the books I describe here and others that you may find in your local library, you can use paintings and works of art that you and your students have around your homes. Calendars with different works of art, pottery and carvings, needlework, greeting cards, and so forth make excellent examples. All of these works of art, both "high" and "folk," help us connect writing with our everyday lives. But there's more. As a prominent cognitive psychologist, Jerome Bruner, affirmed more than four decades ago, art is a mode of knowing. It is the "furthest reach of communication" that frees us from the "forms of instrumental knowing that comprise the center of our awareness... [T]he experience of art nourishes itself, so that having sensed connectedness one is impelled to seek more of it" (Bruner, 1962, p. 73). Art makes us all more human.

Writing About Other People's Photographs

In their classic book *Stop, Look, and Write! Effective Writing Through Pictures* (1964; now unfortunately out of print), Hart Day Leavitt and David Sohn contend that "the way you select words and organize them into whole compositions depends on the way you see human experience. If you do not see anything, you will of course have nothing to say" (p. 7). The teaching of writing, they say, should not be about the teaching of rules but should be about helping writers learn to avoid old abstractions and to capture the "sharp reality in human experience" through specific language and particular details (p. 9). (Again, I'll cite William Carlos Williams's "no ideas but in things.")

Photographs are especially evocative for adult students with limited literacy abilities or limited English skills. They can examine photographs with peers, describe and discuss what they see, and then shape their visual experiences into written texts of various kinds, be they student written or captured in an LEA fashion by the teacher. Marguerite Crowley Weibel (1996) says,

But using pictures as a starting point presents students with a familiar and less intimidating media through which they can stretch their powers of observation and understanding beyond the comfortable world of what they already know to consider ideas and perspectives new to them. (p. 10)

In other words, using photos helps us engage in literacy *education* and not merely in literacy *training*.

BEFORE THE LESSON

1   Gather a collection of different photographs. These might come from book collections in your local library (once again, see Weibel, 1996), photographs that you have gathered from various places, pictures cut from magazines, postcards, and so forth. I strongly recommend that you develop a file of intriguing pictures from magazines and postcards from different locales. (Browse in secondhand stores, or at yard and garage sales.) Try to include a wide variety of images that might promote curiosity; be sure to include people, places, animals, and things.

2   Select one of your pictures as an example. Answer the reporter's 5Ws & H questions: Who, What, Where, When, Why, and How. Then write a simple descriptive paragraph for the picture. Make copies of the 5Ws & H listing and paragraph as an example for your students. I used a picture postcard of an iceberg (see Figure 3):

Who: a beautiful, sculptured-looking iceberg

What: it's floating southward from the arctic

Where: off the coast of Labrador and Newfoundland

Figure 3. Iceberg Postcard

Photo courtesy of Brian Bursey.

When: icebergs drift south in spring and summer, especially in June

Why: the warm weather causes them to break free

How: the icebergs "set sail" southward until they decay and dissolve

Here's the descriptive paragraph:

The iceberg looks like an island in the dark sea, but it is really floating south along the coasts of Labrador and Newfoundland. It has broken off from a much larger iceberg in the Arctic Ocean. It is probably late spring or early summer because that's when the warm weather causes the icebergs to "set sail." It will continue floating south until it further breaks apart and eventually dissolves.

3 After you have a descriptive paragraph based on the 5Ws & H, write a short narrative based on the picture. It might be realistic, serious, funny, or fantastical. Be sure that it is relatively brief in order to serve as a model for students. Make copies for all class members. Here's what I did with the iceberg picture:

Mom ran away on an iceberg. It was three years ago when I was seven. She hasn't come back since.

It happened one June afternoon when the icebergs were sailing down from the North Pole. We were all home. The three youngest kids were squabbling and throwing things at one another. My three older sisters and my big brother were blaring rap music from their CD players. Dad was laid-off then from the fish plant, and he and two of his buddies were drinking beer at the kitchen table while Mom was trying to fix dinner. I was helping her peel potatoes.

When Dad asked Mom to open him another beer, she threw a potato at him and yelled, "That's it! I've had enough!" She took her jacket from the coat tree and walked out the kitchen door down to our dock.

Just then an iceberg came along. We watched Mom get into the run-about, start it, and head out to that floating island. When she got alongside we saw her throw the anchor line and latch onto the ice. She used the rope to pull herself up onto a little ledge on the side of the berg. The last we saw of Mom was her sitting there with her arms folded, and the bottom of her flowered housedress flapping in the breeze.

"She always told me she wanted to travel south," Dad said to his buddies.

4 Notice in my examples that I'm trying to model several things for adult students. First, I want them to see that photographs and pictures of all sorts are visual works worthy of attention and that can serve as springboards to writing. Second, I want them to look closely at the photograph or picture and organize their ideas by using the 5Ws & H structure. Third, once they have a listing of ideas, I want them to see that the list can serve as a basis for different kinds of writing, in this case, a simple descriptive paragraph and a little piece of fantasy. Of course, they can also write poems about their pictures, for example, the lunes, cinquains, and diamantes that we've already explored.

THE LESSON, PART I

1 Share with students your photograph or picture. Explore it with them, asking what they see, what stands out as peculiar to them, and so forth. Then give them your 5Ws & H listing. Tell them as you examined the picture you organized what you saw by making notations under the Who, What, Where, When, Why, and How. Ask them to study the picture and see if there's anything they might be able to add to your listing.

2 Distribute copies of your descriptive paragraph. Read it to students, and then ask them to read it with you a second time. Explain how you used your 5Ws & H list as a basis for your paragraph but that as you were writing you didn't limit yourself to the list.

3 Distribute your narrative based on the picture. Read it to the students, and then have them read it with you a second time. Highlight how the picture might serve as a catalyst for several different types of writing. Explain how you used your imagination to construct a little narrative, or story, based on the picture.

4 At this point in the lesson, if you have time and students are interested in the photograph or picture that you selected, help them as a whole class generate another story based on it by using an LEA format. Typically, however, I skip this option due to time constraints and move right to the next step.

5 Divide students into partners or small groups of three, again providing support for your ELLs. Distribute to each group a selection of photographs or pictures; be sure that each group has a variety of interesting items to look at and discuss. Ask the group members to select one item that they all like.

6 Once the group has an item selected, ask the students to explore it closely and talk about it. Emphasize the 5Ws & H. For example, Who is doing something? What is being done? Where is it being done? When is it being done? Why is it being done? How is it being done? Ask each group to display its picture and to describe it to the rest of the class using the 5Ws & H. Encourage all members of the group to participate in the sharing, however limited their contribution might be.

7 After all of the groups have shared, ask them to brainstorm a brief narrative, or story, about the photo. Refer back to your example. Ask one member of the group to serve as the scribe or secretary. For this first draft, stress to students that they should be concerned with creating an interesting story and not with spelling. Circulate and assist where necessary. Following is a typical example generated by a group of students who were working with a photo of a woman baking bread.

> I was making biscuits. The dough had been mixed, rested, and now was ready to be rolled out. As I picked up my rolling pin I hummed a little tune.
>
> I gently pressed the dough down with my rolling pin. Back and forth across the dough I rolled until it was a half-inch thick. Then I turned to get my biscuit cutter.

Suddenly, out of the hole in the handle of the rolling pin came one, two, three, four little mice. They jumped on the dough and started to do some kind of dance, like a square dance. I got in the spirit and started humming along.

Quickly it was over. The mice took off, and I was left to clean up and mix a new batch of biscuits.

Notice how my iceberg fantasy inspired this group of students. I can't stress strongly enough the importance of teacher writing and modeling.

8 Once groups have rough drafts ask them to share with the whole class.

9 The groups can continue to work on their drafts if they'd like during subsequent meetings.

10 Ask students to bring in for the next class meeting any interesting photographs or pictures that they have at home and about which they'd like to write.

THE LESSON, PART 2

1 Review with students the picture exploration, discussion, listing 5Ws & H, and so on from the last class meeting. If any of the groups have done further work on their stories, have them share with the class. If you have written another story about a different picture, share it.

2 Ask students to share any photographs or pictures they brought in. (Have plenty of photographs and pictures available for those students who for whatever reason did not bring any.)

3 Have each student select one picture that she'd like to talk and write about. Pair students and have them share their pictures using the 5Ws & H structure. They can also jot down words and phrases for the questions as they are sharing.

4 After sharing orally, students can begin first drafts of the stories about their pictures. These stories can be fiction or nonfiction. Circulate and assist where needed. Follow an LEA format for those ELLs and less proficient native English speakers who might need assistance. Your most competent students can also help with ELLs.

5 Rough drafts should be shared before the end of the class meeting, and time during subsequent class sessions should be devoted to polishing the picture stories. These then can be collected along with copies of the photographs and pictures into a class book for future reading and enjoyment.

KEEPING ELLs IN MIND

Informal exploration and discussion among peers is especially important for your ELLs. It provides what Stephen Krashen (1982) calls comprehensible input, does not put ELLs on the defensive, and does not raise their level of anxiety.

WRAP UP

1   In her study of literacy in American lives, Deborah Brandt (2001) notes that "across generations, school-based writing was widely associated with pain, belittlement, and perplexity" (p. 164). Moreover, writing seemed to have had lesser importance than reading in literacy education: "Writing overall seems more associated with troubles. There were more accounts of getting into trouble with writing than with reading and about using writing as a response to trouble" (p. 167). Writing about photographs and pictures, particularly those of a personal nature, can help to obviate some of the negative attitudes adults bring into the literacy classroom. Talking and writing about pictures can be fun or serious depending upon the students' interests and needs. (Paulo Freire, 1970, and his followers, for example, used pictures as a critical and political literacy tool to help adults examine and act on their own social environments.)

2   Adults with limited literacy skills, whether native English speakers or ELLs, live in a visual world. They and we all are surrounded with countless images every day. Thus, the more we can include such images in our literacy lessons the better we will be able to connect the adult classroom with the adults' worlds.

3   Encourage those students who have children to try the same kind of photograph writing activity with their children at home.

Writing About Our Own Photographs

Rena Soifer and her colleagues (1990) have stressed the importance of providing opportunities for adult literacy students to write about things that are important to them and then having appreciative audiences both in and out of the classroom for their writing: "Adults can share their writings with others in and out of class, both to grow in self-esteem and to become better writers" (p. 59). Combining photography with writing fosters this sense of self-esteem among most adults and furthermore offers them multiple ways of making meaning and sharing it with others. In their sourcebook *Multiple Intelligences and Adult Literacy: A Sourcebook for Practitioners* (2004) Julie Viens and Silja Kallenbach describe the importance of developing lessons and activities that tap into adults' different ways of learning and knowing. They cite various examples of how students used drawing and photography to represent what they had learned.

Photography has long been used in different writing projects with young adults and children. The Foxfire collection of oral histories gathered by high school students in rural Georgia, USA, includes hundreds of photographs taken by the students as integral complements to their written texts. (See, for example, Eliot Wigginton, 1972, and the many other Foxfire books.) Wendy Ewald's *I Wanna Take Me a Picture: Teaching Photography and Writing to Children* (2002) describes how she has helped children around the world learn about themselves and their communities by having them take photographs and then write about them. Alas, very little has been written about the use of photography with adult literacy students. Julie Viens and Silja Kallenbach (2004) and Helen Woodrow and I in the brief article "Oral Histories in the Adult Literacy Program" (2001) offer some possible strategies.

In her now-classic study, *On Photography* (1977), the late Susan Sontag wrote that any photograph "has multiple meanings":

> The ultimate wisdom of the photographic image is to say, "There is the surface. Now think— or rather feel, intuit—what is beyond it, what the reality must be like if it looks this way." Photographs, which cannot themselves explain anything, are inexhaustible invitations to deduction, speculation, and fantasy. (p. 20)

This lesson fosters photography and writing as complementary means of deducing, speculating, and fantasizing. In it, adult students take photographs of their immediate contexts and the people and things that are important to them and then use those photographs as the basis for different kinds of writing.

BEFORE THE LESSON

1 Depending upon your particular situation, you'll need to gather cameras for your students' use. You can do this in several ways. First, ask your students if they have access to cameras, either digital or film; typically I have found that many if not most do, including cell phones that take photographs. Second, check to see if your adult literacy center or program has cameras available for use. Third, if the program doesn't have any cameras, check to see if there are funds which might be used to purchase inexpensive one-time use disposal cameras. Fourth, check to see if your local public library has cameras to check out. Fifth, if necessary, ask your students if they can contribute to the purchase of disposable cameras. Last, if you personally own one or more cameras, you might be willing to let students use it or them. The key thing is that students have a camera with which to take photographs of things that are important to them at home, in the local community, at work, and so forth. Digital cameras are ideal for writing purposes. Students can take photographs, download and print them immediately, and then begin their writing. They do not have to wait for the photographs to be developed.

2 Take various photographs that might serve as catalysts for your own writing and as examples for your students. Try to get a diverse selection, for example, photographs of people, objects around your home, your pet(s), scenes from nature (backyard trees and plants), interesting places and signs in your community, and so on. The key thing you want to emphasize is that just as there are innumerable commonplace things to write about, there also are countless things to capture with a camera.

3 Select at least two of your photographs and brainstorm lists of words and phrases as you carefully explore them. Use the reporter's 5Ws & H.

4 Compose a brief text for each photograph. Try to have a different discourse type for each; in that way you'll model for your students the fact that a photograph offers various opportunities for writing, and, as Sontag (1977) has noted, for multiple meanings. I've included two examples. The first shows two photographs I took of wild cherries and the little poems I wrote about them (see Figure 4). The second example is about my dog, Molly. She is a black Labrador Retriever (see Figure 5).

THE LESSON, PART I

1 Introduce the lesson by explaining to your students that they'll be exploring ways of using photography to further foster and improve their writing. Ask how many students take photographs on a regular basis or even occasionally. Have volunteers share the following information: What kinds of pictures do they take? What kinds of cameras might they use? Determine how many students have access to a camera.

2 Talk briefly on the value of taking photographs and then using them for different kinds of writing. Stress the fact that looking through the viewfinder of a camera necessarily helps us limit the world and concentrate on particulars, leading to the same kind of close attention that a poet or novelist gives her subject. Moreover, highlight the fact that by photographing the same thing from many different angles and distances we often are able to see the thing from various perspectives.

3 Have available at this first session at least one camera for each group of three students. (If you have digital cameras and a printer readily available, then you can show the students' photographs before the end of the class.) Divide students into groups of three and give each group a camera. (If you have enough cameras for partner teams,

---

Figure 4. Wild Cherries Photographs and Poems

The cherries burn
With summer
In the sun's rays

The cherries alive
In summer
A blackbird circles

Figure 5. Molly Photograph and Narrative

A neighbor kid once said, "Molly, she's a dolly!" Well, that's true, some of the time. Like almost all Labrador Retrievers she's a great companion in the woods, on the jogging trail, and in the backyard where she'll fetch balls for hours it seems. At two-and-a-half years of age she has boundless energy, and she loves to play with any stranger who approaches her. The problem, however, is that she tends to jump on people, and at 65 pounds she can knock an unprepared person off his feet. She also likes to dig in the vegetable garden during the summer. I guess she's like most of us, too: a combination of both positive and negative traits.

that's even better.) Demonstrate or have one or more of the experienced students demonstrate how to use the particular cameras: just point and shoot, use a flash, how to focus, and so on.

4   Distribute around the room simple objects that can be photographed. I have used such things as objects from nature (e.g., leaves, pine cones, branches, driftwood, odd-shaped rocks), fruits and vegetables (e.g., eggplants, artichokes, different kinds of mushrooms, pineapples), or any other things that you think might provide a variety of interesting photographs.

5   Model for students how you might approach one of the objects with the camera by viewing it from different angles and distances. If you have any experienced photographers in your group, let them do the modeling; let them be the teachers! Have students look through their cameras' viewfinders at the same object. Do not take any photographs at this point in time. Discuss which angles and distances might result in interesting photographs.

6   Ask students to circulate around the room and to select two items that they would like to photograph. Tell each trio or partner team to explore possible shots, and then have each member of the group take photographs of the same two objects.

7   If the students are using digital cameras and if you have ready access to a printer—and if you have enough time—you can download and print the photographs for examination. If not, you can have them for the next class session.

8 Share as examples your two photographs and the complementary writing. Briefly explain the process you followed.

9 Instruct students to take interesting photographs in their home environments, for example, in their own home, surrounding community, place of employment, and so forth before the next class meeting. Explain that their photographs could be of people, animals, or objects. Tell them to photograph things that they will want to write about. (Depending on the kinds of cameras available and the students' access to their own cameras, you might have to limit the number of shots they should take.)

THE LESSON, PART 2

1 Display the photographs taken in the last class by trios or partners. Ask students in each group to discuss which photograph they'd like to write about. Once they have selected a photograph, have them do the following while you circulate and assist where needed.

2 Look closely at the photograph; note even the most insignificant things in it.

3 Brainstorm a list of words and phrases that describe the object in the photograph.

4 Arrange the brainstormed list under the reporter's 5Ws & H.

5 Using the 5Ws & H, write a short descriptive paragraph about the photograph. Here's a brief piece that two students wrote about some sprays of lilacs:

> These lilacs are pink and purple in color. Up very close they look like little dancers. Their strong smell reminds us of springtime.

6 Have students share their brief descriptive pieces and ask for appreciations.

7 After students have shared, ask them to return to the photograph and begin a vignette about it, that is, to tell a story about the picture. Here's the lilac vignette:

> These lilacs are like the two huge bushes that were in our front yard when I was a girl. I discovered between those bushes there was a big space. When I went in, it was like a little room. Once I was inside the branches closed and it was very secret. It was really nice when the lilacs were in bloom.

8 Have students share the drafts of their photograph vignettes. Tell them they can continue working on them before the next class meeting or in future classes. Inform them that you'll have copies of the photographs they took at home ready the next time you meet. (You might already have them if the students had them developed themselves or if they used digital cameras and you were able to print them during this second part of the lesson. For students with limited incomes, you may need to be responsible for developing the photos.)

THE LESSON, PART 3

1 Distribute and share the photographs that students have taken. Allow time for individuals to discuss why they took particular photographs, the people in them, and so forth. (You might want to use the reporter's 5Ws & H as an organizing structure for sharing. I don't think this simple format can be used enough.) This oral sharing will serve as part of the prewriting.

2 Ask students as individuals or as partners to follow the same process as in Part 2 of the lesson, that is, select one of their photographs that they might want to write about, jot down a list of words or phrases, and so forth. Have students write a descriptive piece or a poem. Circulate and assist where necessary. Here's a poem by Ray that he wrote about a picture of his mother.

> My Mother is a wonderful person.
> She is the nicest you want to meet.
> She is so loving and kind,
> When something goes wrong
> You can call her up
> And talk to her about it.
> She is the best Mom
> You want her to be.

And here is part of a prose piece by Ledinor that accompanies a picture of his son:

> Every night I help him with his writing and spelling. We play all kinds of games. He is doing very good in school. That makes me happy because I can help him just a little bit. My goal is to help my son with lots more. We listen to tape stories, and that is very good for me and him.

3 Ask students to share their working drafts and encourage them to continue working on their photograph vignettes and poems at home. Allow for future class time to write, draft, edit, and publish final copies.

KEEPING ELLs IN MIND

Encouraging ELLs to capture in photographs and writing their own lived and storied contexts fosters success and adults' sense of self as language users. Moreover, it honors them and their family, friends, and extended community. This is very different from having adult ELLs write about a picture in a workbook that is unrelated to their communities and their lives.

WRAP UP

1   In her study of adult learners' lives and how their "literate subjectivities shift across different domains of literate experiences," Rebecca Rogers (2004) concludes that "conceptualizing adults' literate lives as storied selves helps us to reimagine all of the places where they are successful and to build from these places" (p. 296). Rogers's research highlights the fact that adults' sense of themselves as individuals and as literate beings changed according to particular contexts. For example, when they were involved with their children's literacy and learning they saw themselves as active and competent. On the other hand, when they reflected on their past schooling experiences they perceived themselves to be passive and less than competent. Accordingly, as much as possible we need to help adults connect to those times and places in which they felt successful. Encouraging them to explore their own lives and communities in photographs and writing fosters a sense of personal control, expertise, and competence.

2   Andrew Pates and Maggie Evans (1994) describe adult writing workshops in a British context and note that "[p]hotography and other media may contribute substantially by providing further stimuli for the writing" (p. 146). Video and audio equipment might extend the use of photographs that I describe here. For example, a video might encourage storyboarding and script writing. Whether photographing with cameras or cell phones, videotaping, audiotaping, or generating images on computers, by helping adults connect their writing and reading to a variety of media we are helping them gain greater control over their literate lives. This should be our role as literacy educators.

Writing About Art in Everyday Life

In *Art as Experience* (1934) John Dewey dismisses the notion that art is something separate from our daily lives. Instead, he says that he wants to recover "the continuity of esthetic experience with normal processes of living" (p. 10). He goes on to say that "we can discover how the work of art develops and accentuates what is characteristically valuable in things of everyday enjoyment" (p. 11). Dewey was concerned with how we can make art an integral part of everyday life and not something for an elite minority. Art, he believed, has social roots and a social value. He emphasized that an individual must actively engage a work of art and thus in a very real sense help to create it: "Without an act of recreation the object is not perceived as a work of art" (p. 54). Louise Rosenblatt's (1978) transactional theory of reading based upon Dewey's work is widely known among literacy educators. Just as Dewey maintains that a work of art does not exist without individuals who perceive it and help to re-create it in any number of ways, Rosenblatt contends that any text does not really mean anything until individuals transact with it. A painting and likewise a short story, novel, or poem might have as many meanings as there are viewers or readers. In her terminology it is the individual reader's transaction with a particular text that creates the "poem."

We encounter many different kinds of art daily, most of which we take for granted and do not consider as "art." Print, television, and Internet advertisements; billboards; the packaging of products in the supermarket; and logos on everything from shoes, baseball caps, shirts, and soft drink cans all have been created by commercial artists with the intent of convincing us to buy something or otherwise influencing us in some way.

The purpose of this lesson is to highlight these everyday art objects by calling attention to them through different kinds of writing. Writing about environmental artwork, for example, on a cereal box or a trademark logo on a baseball cap, is not only fun but also offers adults an almost limitless source of things about which to write. Moreover, it helps them—and us as literacy educators—to become more attentive to the world around us, and it is this attention that helps make interesting writers.

BEFORE THE LESSON

1 Gather a number of examples of everyday art from newspaper advertisements, magazine layouts, grocery products, T-shirts, and so forth. Try to include a varied collection of interesting visual images from which your students can choose.

2 Select two or three examples and write accompanying poems, vignettes, tales, dramatic scripts, and so on for each. You will use these as models for your students. Following are some examples that I wrote. First is a cinquain (described in Chapter 3).

> Item: a can of Green Giant sweet corn with the giant standing in the middle of a green corn field and a mound of yellow corn sweeping across the label.

> Corn
> Sweet whole
> Growing greening glowing
> I love yellow niblets
> Maiz

I used the words and images on the label for the cinquain. Next is a short tale (described in Chapter 6):

> Item: a colorful newspaper ad for Trail Mix bars that shows a family of wallabies inside an automobile heading out on a vacation. The caption reads, "You won't find a trail mix bar made with high fructose corn syrup on this Wallaby family road trip."
>
> What was junior thinking in the backseat while clutching his baseball? Why did he feel an urge to throw it at someone? Was it because he had been playing with a dingo? Was it because he had been dreaming of Tasmanian devils? Was his wallaby father really his father, or had his mother had an affair with a devil while growing up in Tasmania? Perhaps he would get some answers on this road trip.

Last is an entry from my personal reflection journal (described in Chapter 1).

Item: a T-shirt with a spiky-rayed sun shining from a blue sky with two white clouds upon purple mountains. The printing reads, "Take a Hike. Sabino Canyon. Tucson Arizona." On the sides of the images are the names of the various hiking trails in Sabino Canyon.

Hiked the Phone Line Trail all the way to Stop 9. Saw no one else on the trail this early in the morning. Thought I saw a javelina in a side canyon, or maybe it was a coyote. The desert is lush and green after the monsoon rains. The saguaro cacti seem more lordly than ever.

3 Make copies of your writing for your students. (You should be able to get the two or three pieces you wrote on a single page.)

THE LESSON, PART I

1 Distribute the everyday art examples among your students. Ask them to look at the images, designs, and words. Ask them to think about what makes these items attractive and effective in terms of getting people to buy the products or notice the T-shirt designs, and so on. Encourage responses and discussion. For example, a Spanish-speaking woman commented that it was not only the green giant on the corn can that grabbed her attention, but the fact that all of the writing was in both English and Spanish ("Whole Kernel Sweet Corn/Maiz dulce de granos enteros").

2 Explain that this sort of everyday art is all around us, but often we don't pay attention to it and, especially, the way it might affect us in terms of what we purchase, think, and so forth.

3 Distribute the copies of the texts that you wrote to accompany the two or three items about which you wrote. Show the items and read the brief poems or prose pieces. Ask the adults to follow along as you read. Read each piece at least twice. Encourage appreciations. Describe how you went about choosing the kind of text you'd write for each item. For example, I chose a cinquain for the corn can because I saw it would be easy to use the actual words on the can label. Brainstorm other possible kinds of texts for your items. List them on the dry-erase board or chart paper.

4 Ask the adults to select one of your items about which to write a whole-class piece. Brainstorm words, phrases, and ideas. List them. Using an LEA format, transcribe the class text(s). Here are two additional poems generated by different groups of students, the first a lune (described in Chapter 3) and the second an apology poem (also described in Chapter 3):

A green man
Standing in a hilly field
Mountain of corn

This is just to say
I ate the can of corn
Leaving you none

> Sorry
> It was
> "Naturalmente Mas Dulce"

5 Divide your students into partners or trios with ELLs matched with native English speakers. Have them select one of the everyday art items you brought to class. Tell them to look closely at the images, coloring, words, and so forth. Suggest they discuss how the art might (or does) affect them. Have one person in each team act as a scribe and jot down words and ideas.

6 After all of the teams have had an opportunity to talk about their items, have them share their ideas with the class. Often this opportunity to share will generate other ideas.

7 At this point you have two options: Each team can choose the kind of accompanying text it wants to write, or you can decide as a class to all write a particular kind of text, for example, a lune, vignette, and so on. Have the teams compose a first draft while you circulate and assist where needed. Following are a couple of student examples. The first is a lune for a cereal box:

> Crunchy cereal puffs
> Healthy foods sparked by passion
> It's very good

Lunes and cinquains tend to work well for labels because adults can use the actual words describing the items, and the language is quite often "rich" in terms of description. This is a natural way to use environmental print to help adults expand their reading and writing vocabularies.

The next example is a prose vignette (described in Chapter 2) for a T-shirt that has an outline map of Iowa with a star that designates the town of Britt and above the map in large print is "National Hobo Convention":

> What in the world do hoboes do at a convention? Where do they all come from? Maybe they just sit around campfires and tell stories. Maybe they talk about where they might go next. They must be a strange and interesting bunch of people. Maybe someday we'll go to Britt to see them.

8 After all of the teams have a first draft, share them as a whole class. Encourage appreciations. If the team members choose, they can copy their texts for their personal folders.

9 Ask students to look around their homes, places of work, or neighborhoods for some interesting everyday artwork about which they might want to write. Offer additional suggestions if you think it's necessary, for example, soft drink cans, various labels on different bottles of water, and so on. Ask them to bring one or more pieces to the next class meeting. Suggest that if they get a chance, they should try a piece of writing at home.

THE LESSON, PART 2

1   Review what was done during the previous class meeting. Share any new writing that you've done on a piece of everyday art. Ask the students if they had a chance to do any writing. Encourage sharing and appreciations.

2   Ask students to share any examples of art that they brought in. (If not all of the students have brought something in, be sure to have a collection on hand from the first class or new examples that you've gathered.)

3   Have each student select one piece of everyday art about which he'd like to write. Depending on the kinds of writing your students have been doing up to this point in time, either have them determine individually what sort of text to write or decide as a whole class for everyone to write a particular kind of poem, vignette, tale, and so forth.

4   Have partners first talk out their ideas and jot down words and phrases they might use. Encourage partners to offer suggestions to each other about their individual pieces of everyday art.

5   When they think they are ready, have students begin their individual first drafts. Circulate and assist with spelling if necessary; offer encouragement and ideas if adults seem stalled.

6   When students have written first drafts or at least have begun drafts, stop and have them voluntarily share what they've produced. Once again, encourage appreciations and suggestions among class members.

7   During subsequent class meetings allow time for students to continue working on final drafts of their everyday art pieces. Here are a couple examples of students' final drafts. The first from Anne is a lune, and the second from Nick is a personal reflection.

Item: a label from a jar of strawberry preserves

> Bright red strawberries
> Thunder rain growing in sunshine
> Jam on bread

Item: a grocery flyer for a special sale on spaghetti sauce
The spaghetti my wife made for dinner was real good. It had lots of sausage in it. My slurping was fine, and my wife said that there'd be more washing to do when I was done.

8   Encourage students to continue writing about everyday art at home and with their children as a joint project. Post the finished pieces of writing and the accompanying pieces of artwork around the classroom or collect them in a class booklet. Perhaps there's an opportunity to publish them in an online forum. There are various Internet sites on which adult students can read other literacy students' writing or

publish their own work. For reading try the Ohio Literacy Resource Center's collection titled *Beginnings* from the Ohio Writers' Conference (archon.educ.kent.edu/). The National Adult Literacy Database (NALD) from Canada has a bounty of student writing from adult literacy programs across that country (www.nald.ca/index.htm). Two sites to which students can submit their work are the Poetry Scriber (www.poetry scriber.com) and SMITH Magazine (www.smithmag.net). Poetry Scriber highlights poetry of all sorts, and SMITH Magazine site has a number of engaging story projects, for example, six-word memoirs.

KEEPING ELLs IN MIND

1 This lesson is particularly useful for ELLs because it allows them to connect to everyday things in their surrounding environment through speaking, listening, reading, and writing. The visuals on grocery products, signs, clothing, and so on can serve as catalysts for their learning the language that accompanies these items.

2 Using an LEA format (as a whole class and, if necessary, with you and an individual) will provide ELLs with a model of spoken and written English and support for their developing literacy abilities.

3 ELLs can add new vocabulary items to their personal word banks, dictionaries, writing folders, or word lists. If a particular item is in two languages (such as the Green Giant corn can label) and one of the languages is the student's native tongue, she can pair some of the words, for example, *corn—maiz, sweet—dulce*.

4 If your students are keeping observation journals as described in Chapter 1, they can jot down any new English words, phrases, or sentences accompanying advertisements, billboards, television commercials, and so on that they encounter in their daily lives. They can share these in class or with you personally, and you can then use them as the basis for additional writing or vocabulary work.

WRAP UP

Writing about everyday art helps adults see that they can write about anything and that their writing can take a variety of forms and lengths. The more you can encourage such close observation of the world among your students and subsequent writing about things in it, the more you will help demystify writing for them.

CHAPTER 6

Fostering Imagination With Fiction

I N CHAPTER 2, I stressed that we are all natural born storytellers who are constantly telling and hearing stories. Weibel (1996) contends that people "crave stories. Stories tell us who we are as individuals and as members of families, social groups, and nations" (p. 76). I have long argued for the importance of stories and fiction in adult literacy education. Fiction enables adults to create unique characters, situations, and events. It fosters imaginative power and control and helps them to become "world makers." As Weibel (1996) asserts, "It is the literature of any culture that tells its stories. Whether they are fiction, folktales, essays, memoirs, letters, or true life accounts, these are the stories that we need to bring to Hattie [an adult student] and to other literacy students" (p. 79).

Adult education, whether it be basic literacy, ELL, or GED preparation, is all too often somber, if not bleak. There is often too little laughter and the joy of goofing around with language. Adults with limited literacy abilities need many opportunities to play with words, sentences, and stories. They need to *experience* the fact through their own reading and writing that literacy is much more than work-related or simply a functional skill. The reading and writing of outrageous stories and tall tales provides them with such experiences. Literacy is immeasurable, so is laughter. James Hillman (1996) observes, "Humor as the word also implies, moistens and softens, giving a common touch; it is anathema to grandiosity, fostering self-reflection and distancing us from self-importance" (pp. 221–222). Indeed, it helps make us more human and it helps us connect with other people.

The current interest in short or "flash" fiction, that is, stories of sometimes only 100 words or less, offers adult literacy educators many fine models to share with their students. (See, for example, *Flash Fiction: Very Short Stories* edited by Thomas, Thomas, and Hazuka, 1992; and Moss's *The World's Shortest Stories: Murder. Love. Horror. Suspense. All This and Much More in the Most Amazing Short Stories Ever Written—Each One Just 55 Words Long!*, 1998.) I have found that folktales, legends, porquoi tales, tall tales, and just plain nonsense stories are enjoyable and useful in the adult classroom. No matter our age or cultural background, we all enjoy imaginative play. Barry Sanders (1994) contends,

The teaching of literacy has to be founded on a curriculum of song, dance, play, and joking, coupled with improvisation and recitation. Students need to hear stories, either made up by the teacher or read aloud. They need to make them up themselves or try to retell them in their own words. (p. 243)

Accordingly, with imaginative play, joking, and nonsense in mind, I present in this chapter three lessons that highlight short fiction: tall tales or outrageous stories, flash fiction from pictures, and scary or ghost stories. An additional lesson focuses on writing imaginative stories in the form of dramatic scripts.

Tall Tales and Other Kinds of Nonsense

We all like to exaggerate at times, stretch the truth, or tell "whoppers." It's fun, and regardless of age, gender, race, or ethnicity, we engage in hyperbole. "Oh, it was hard when I was a kid. We had to walk five miles to school, and it was uphill both ways!" "Talk about eating crawfish! We ate a hundred pounds at one sitting!" "I thought we were goners on the lake during that storm. The waves were at least twenty feet high, and we were in our canoe!" All cultures have tall tales and outrageous folk stories that are readily available for use with adults. A trip to your public library, a search on Google of "tall tales," or a check on Amazon.com will give you some idea of the thousands of available tales. You can select those that you think will be most effective with your particular group of students, from such classic tales as Paul Bunyan, Johnny Appleseed, and Sally Ann Thunder to such lesser known tales as those of African American heroines like Annie Christmas and Native characters such as Otoonah of the Sugpiaq people of the Aleutian Islands. Bruce Springsteen's immensely popular "Seeger Sessions" CD includes a great version of John Henry the steel-driving man (simply titled "John Henry") that is fun to play and use with adults.

BEFORE THE LESSON

1 Read through the lesson and determine how long it might take with your group of adults. Consider any special adaptations you might have to make for your ELLs.

2 Select one or more short tall tales to share with your students. Use those that will resonate with ELLs. Picture books are fine for use with adult literacy students. There are many illustrated tales that provide new and less proficient readers with visual support and cues.

3 Write a short tall tale of your own. Simply take any "normal" situation or incident and exaggerate it in some fashion. Try to include humor in your tale as a model. Make copies for all of your students. Following is one of my examples that I've used a number of times with different groups:

"Ice Fishing on Buffalo Lake"

I was ice fishing last week, and the line pulled so hard that the pole almost flew from my hands.

I couldn't reel the fish an inch, and the rod was being tugged into the hole I had augered. I called for my buddy, and he grabbed me around the waist, but still we couldn't bring up the fish.

We called out to two other guys, and all four of us began to pull. Finally, the nose of the fish peeked through the ice hole—just the nose. It was a muskie, and its head was too big to fit through the hole.

We yelled, and a guy named Ray came with an ax and began to chop a bigger hole. Just when we saw the muskie's huge head, it leaped up and grabbed the ax. It jerked Ray headfirst into the hole. We had to drop the pole and grab his feet to save him from being pulled down into the lake.

Ray came out of the water still holding the ax handle. The muskie had bitten off the ax head. Ray shook his wet, now ice-covered head in wonder. "That's one hell of a fishing lure!" he said.

THE LESSON, PART 1

1 Explain what you'll be doing in the lesson.

2 Ask the students how many know any tall tales, whoppers, or stretching-the-truth stories. (Be sure to explain what you mean by such terms if you have ELLs in your class.) Encourage volunteers to share.

3 Read one or more of the short tall tales that you selected. (I like to use Pecos Bill and Paul Bunyan as classic American examples, "Master Maid" and "Mop Top" tales from Norway, and "Master Man" tales from Nigeria.) Encourage responses and discussion. Read the tale or tales a second time if students seem especially enthused.

4 Brainstorm with the students what makes a tall tale. List on the dry-erase board or chart paper their varied responses. Highlight especially (particularly if they don't) that tall tales typically include exaggeration, humor, and wit. Be sure to save the brainstormed list for Part 2 of the lesson.

5 Distribute copies of your tall tale. Read it aloud and tell the students to follow along. Then read it a second time asking them to join in with you. Ask for responses and appreciations. Explain to students how you went about writing your tale, that is generating ideas, drafting, using dialogue, perhaps emphasizing the use of humor, and so on.

6 Conclude the first part of the lesson by asking students to reread aloud with a partner one or more of the tales you distributed. Be sure to match ELLs with more proficient native English speakers. Circulate and assist where necessary. Tell students to take home the tales and practice reading them.

THE LESSON, PART 2

1 Review by reading aloud one or more of the tall tales from the last meeting. Ask the students to read along with you. Then review the brainstormed list of tall tale characteristics.

2 List ideas for possible group, partner, and individual tall tales. Give the students two options: They can generate ideas or you can provide them with ideas from collections of tall tales. I also like using a combination of student ideas and those from collections. You can determine which option will work best with your students. For example, here are some ideas from Carl Sandburg's poem "The People, Yes" (1970):

> Of the man so tall he must climb a ladder to shave himself...
> Of mosquitoes: one can kill a dog, two of them a man. (p. 492)

And here are a few ideas generated by a group of students:

> Riding a bike and keeping up with a jet plane
> Bowling a perfect game every time
> Strange things while ice fishing [obviously a result of my tall tale]
> Extreme hot or cold weather, unbelievable storms, and so on

3 As a whole class, select one of the possible tall tale topics and brainstorm ideas for a short sketch. Act as a scribe and use an LEA format. List the ideas on the dry-erase board or chart paper. As an example, here's a list students brainstormed for another ice fishing tale:

> ice houses
>
> big fish
>
> dogs
>
> Labs
>
> Pit Bulls
>
> ice holes
>
> dogs swimming
>
> people swimming
>
> ladies watching TV
>
> men drinking schnapps
>
> surprises

And here is the group tall tale:

> Two men were in their fish house fishing and drinking peppermint schnapps. They had a black Lab with them, a big one. Suddenly the Lab spotted a giant walleye in the hole.

It leaped in after the fish and swam to the next fish house. It came up out of the fishing hole right where two women were watching a portable TV. They were so surprised and scared that they broke right through the plywood door with the Lab right after them!

4 Following an LEA format, read and reread the tall tale as you write it. After the students have a version that they like, reread the tale as a whole group and then ask for volunteers.

5 Have students select one of the brainstormed ideas (or any others that might come to mind) and, working with a partner or alone, try writing a first draft of their own tall tale. If necessary, match ELLs with more proficient native English speakers. Circulate and assist where needed, by helping students generate their tales and suggesting possible vocabulary, spelling, and so forth. Following are two student tales that I especially like:

I lived in Mississippi on a farm. The trouble with Mississippi is it gets hot! One day it got so hot when I looked at the thermometer it said 120 degrees, 150 degrees. Then it busted. I looked down at my feet and they were smoking!

—by James

I caught a 150-pound sturgeon one time on a no-see visible line. I reeled it in with the no-see reel while the fish was flying by high in the hot air.

—by Raymond

6 After individuals and partners have written first drafts, encourage volunteers to share them. Instruct students to continue working on their tall tales at home and provide time in future classes for them to polish their tales. Have students add these tales to their writing folders. They might also be collected into a separate booklet.

KEEPING ELLs IN MIND

Tall tales and outrageous humorous stories foster imaginative uses of language among all students, native speakers of English and ELLs alike. They inform second-language learning with play—something, alas, that is too often missing in adult classrooms. As Ann Berthoff (1981) contends, "To begin with meaning is to begin with the imagination—a natural power—which brings form to consciousness. That is a fairly good description of pedagogical purpose" (p. 92).

WRAP UP

A valuable resource for reading and writing with adult students is *Reader's Digest*. A typical issue contains a wide variety of topics. Most articles are short, and the writing tends to be clear and clean without being "dumbed down." Especially relevant in the exploration of short fiction and humor are the regular features titled "Life in These United States," "All in a Day's Work," and "Humor in Uniform." These sections contain funny stories written by readers, and there are usually four in each section. The only guidelines are that the funny stories must be original and less than 100 words. The stories must be submitted online. I have found that most people are excited about submitting work that might be published, especially because the magazine pays US$300.00 for any story accepted!

Flash Fiction From Pictures

Pictures from magazines and newspapers offer adults a wealth of ideas about which to write. Pairing two or three related or unrelated pictures together can help individuals, partners, small groups, or the whole class compose short pieces of flash fiction that have beginnings, middles, and ends. These fictional sketches might be funny, serious, or mysterious. For example, here's a whole-class piece that was written using an LEA format after putting together three pictures: a man with long hair, a magazine picture of cows grazing in a pasture, and a picture of a baldheaded man. The adults in the class discussed the pictures, then brainstormed possible conflicts, sequences of action, vocabulary, and conclusions. I wrote their ideas on chart paper and then drafted the story as they dictated it. I encouraged them to try and keep the story under 100 words. After editing and paring, they got it down to 117 words. Here is the final edited version:

> Tony had long, beautiful hair, and he was conceited. His best friend Pete decided to play a trick on him. He told Tony he had read a science article that proved cow manure was the best thing to keep your hair thick and free from ever falling out.
>
> So Tony said, "I'll give it a try!"
>
> He went out to a farm and collected fresh cow manure. He took it home and rubbed it in his hair. He let it set overnight.
>
> When he awoke in the morning and took a shower, all of his hair came off!
>
> "I never told you to keep it on your head all night," Pete laughed when he saw him.

BEFORE THE LESSON

1 Read through the lesson and determine how long it might take with your students. Consider the special needs of any ELLs you might have in class.

2 Assemble a large collection of pictures from magazines, newspapers, advertising fliers of various kinds, and so forth. They do not have to be mounted or laminated; simply cut them out from the different texts. (Whenever I'm reading, say, a newspaper and come across an interesting, weird, or funny picture, I cut it out and add it to my collection.) Your pictures should be diverse and offer possibilities for many different kinds of stories. If you have students working together in groups of three, each group should have at least 10 pictures from which to choose. Thus, in a class of 15 students, try to have a collection of 50 pictures or so.

3 If you have a copy of Steve Moss's *The World's Shortest Stories* (1998) select one of the 55-word stories to use as an example of flash fiction. (I personally like and have found to be effective catalysts "Split Personality," p. 45, "Rites of Passage," p. 69, and "The Bus Station," p. 160.) If you don't have the book, use one of the stories from this lesson.

4 Select three pictures and write a short fictional tale about them. Try to limit the number of words you use. (The value of flash fiction, 55-word stories, and other short texts is that these forms highlight for adult writers, experienced or otherwise, the fact that a piece of writing does not have to be long to be good. All too often students of whatever age and ability assume that quantity equals quality. Moreover, for adults who have not been successful with writing in the past or for whom English is not a native language, composing brief stories provides a sense of accomplishment and competency.) I've found that humorous, incongruous, and weird stories work best. (Again, *The World's Shortest Stories* has plenty of these.) Following is a piece of flash fiction that I wrote based on pictures of a Bose CD player, a mattress advertisement, and a picture of a pizza:

> Once he got his new Bose CD player and Sleep Number mattress, all he wanted to do was stay in bed, listen to music, and eat take-out pizzas.
> "You'll lose your job," his wife said.
> He did and didn't care.
> "You'll get fat," she complained.
> He did and didn't care.
> "I'll leave you," she warned.
> She did, and she didn't care.

THE LESSON, PART I

1 Explain what you'll be doing in the lesson.

2 Share with students the example of flash fiction you've selected. Ask students to follow along as you read it. Read the story a second time, and then read it a third time and ask the students to join in. Encourage responses. Typical reactions are, "It's short." Stress the fact that stories don't have to be long.

3 Distribute copies of the story that you wrote and show the pictures you used as the catalyst. Read your story and have the students follow along. Then read it as a whole group in a choral manner. Explain how you went about writing your piece of flash fiction, that is, grouping the pictures, brainstorming possible ideas, jotting down words and phrases, considering dialogue, determining if you wanted your story to be serious, funny, or strange, and so forth. This process of thinking aloud provides adults with an understanding and model of how writers think and work.

4 Ask a couple of adults to randomly select two pictures from your collection. Tell them to pick pictures that are very different. Once they have selected the pictures pass them around the class in order for all students to have a close look. Then tell them that it'll be fun if the class tries to write a short fictional story based on the two pictures. Suggest that they try to keep it under 100 words if possible.

5 Display the pictures by attaching them to the dry-erase board or wall or by simply having them circulate among the class. Have the students brainstorm words, phrases, and ideas about the pictures. Make a list of their ideas. After they have generated the list, encourage further brainstorming about a possible plot, that is, a story with a beginning, middle, end, and a conflict of some sort that drives it along. This usually takes some time and guidance by the instructor if the students haven't written from pictures before.

6 Once the class has generated ideas and possible story lines, ask them to construct a story while you write it using an LEA format. Read and reread the story as they dictate it and encourage them to add or change things in the process of writing. When they have a draft with which they are comfortable, read it together a couple of times. Ask if they would like to make any additions. Count the number of words and ask if there's anything they might leave out in order to have as short a story as possible. Tell them that you'll make copies of the story for the next class meeting and that then they'll have an opportunity to write some more flash fiction from pictures in small groups. Here's an example of an edited class story (written using an LEA format) based on a picture of a newspaper and another of a pretty woman. The students titled it "Love":

> I was working in the printing plant on the conveyor belt where the newspaper comes down. One day I got a note that came down on the conveyor belt from one of the women on the line. She asked if I wanted to go out with her. I wrote "Yes," and signed the note. It went back around the line.
>
> I went on a date with Mary that weekend, and then we got serious. Finally we got married, and we have been married now for 20 years.
>
> The funny thing is that Mary never wrote that note. Another woman did. Mary just happened to pick up my response. I'm glad for her interception!

THE LESSON, PART 2

1 Distribute copies of the students' flash fiction from the previous lesson. Read it aloud and ask the students to follow along. Then read it together as a whole class a second time. Ask if there are any individuals or partners who would like to read it a third time.

2 Ask students to form teams of three or four. Have ELLs work with native English speakers. Distribute your collection of pictures among the class and allow time for each team to select two or three pictures about which they would like to write a short fictional story. (I encourage funny or weird stories the first time around.)

3 Once students have selected their pictures, have them *tell* stories about them. Suggest that they try to tell two or three different stories and that they try arranging the pictures in different sequences. This play with possible stories and sequences helps adults see that there are always alternatives when composing a piece of writing, especially a piece of imaginative fiction. Moreover, it helps them better understand that one of the best ways to engage in prewriting is to talk about what it is we're going to write.

4 After the teams have invented stories about their pictures, ask for volunteers to share the pictures and briefly tell one story. This oral sharing among the whole class might generate further ideas for students.

5 After sharing, instruct each team to write down one of their stories. Each team should select one member to act as the secretary or scribe. Tell students not to worry about spelling, punctuation, and so forth on this first draft but simply to try to get the story down on paper. Circulate and assist where needed.

6 If there is time have volunteers share the written drafts of their stories. Encourage appreciations from other class members. If time runs out, instruct students to save their pictures and story draft until the next class meeting.

THE LESSON, PART 3

1 Have each team reread and review its pictures and the draft of the written story. Tell them to discuss any new ideas they might have about the pictures and story and to make any changes they'd like on the draft.

2 Ask for volunteers to share the stories and encourage appreciations.

3 Depending upon your students' stories, abilities, and needs, explicitly teach a short minilesson on one aspect of brief fiction writing. For example you might want to refer to the "rules" for writing a 55-word story:

> So although some may have a more complex definition of just what constitutes a "story," for our purposes, a story is a story only if it contains the following four elements: 1) a setting; 2) a character or characters; 3) a conflict; and 4) resolution. (Moss, 1998, p. 219)

You might also focus on opening "hooks" or surprise endings, more interesting word choice, use of a print thesaurus or an online version, and so forth. Here are a couple of student revisions.

> More interesting opening:
> The doctor said to use canned milk. (Original)
> "Carnation canned milk does strange things on eczema," the doctor smiled. (Revised)

> More effective resolution:
> And he wasn't quite sure what had happened. (Original)
> "My, isn't this interesting!" he scratched his head. (Revised)

4 Once students have drafts with which they are happy, make copies for their writing folders. Encourage students to try writing such imaginative pieces based on pictures at home, particularly with their children. They can subsequently work on these stories to polish their punctuation, grammar skills, and so forth (as we'll explore in Chapter 7). A collection of these flash fiction picture stories can also be collected and bound for all class members.

KEEPING ELLs IN MIND

1 Encouraging ELLs to tell and listen to stories with native English speakers in small groups fosters the "forgetting principle" (Krashen, 1982, p. 66) in which they can safely try out the language without fear of making mistakes. Moreover, if they are shy, reticent, or possess very limited English ability, they can simply listen to their English-speaking group members. The pictures will give them something concrete with which to follow along.

2 Oral storytelling is central to various cultural groups. Fostering oral telling as a pre-writing strategy will complement and acknowledge particular cultural practices.

3 Whole-class and small-group reading and rereading of the several stories will support the ELLs in their own reading of the texts. Subsequent rereading with a partner will help the students gain more confidence and will foster fluency.

4 Using an LEA format to construct whole-class and small-group texts encourages ELLs to try out their (however limited) English by adding a word, words, or sentences to the flash fiction stories.

5 If your ELLs are keeping a vocabulary notebook or word bank cards (which I strongly recommend), have them select three new words from their group story and write each word on a separate small index card. On the other side of the card they can write the complete sentence in which the word appeared. They might also write the word in their home language. These words and sentences can be reviewed with you or with a partner at each class meeting; moreover, they can be practiced at home.

WRAP UP

1 I like having adults write short fictional pieces from pictures because they (the pictures) provide something concrete to think about and with which to play. A variation on this picture writing is to ask your students to take out two or three things from their pockets, wallets, purses, and so forth and arrange them in some fashion to tell an imaginative story. For example, I might take out a pen, key, and five-dollar bill and begin my story thus:

> I was out hiking with the Prince of Norway the other weekend, and he gave me a key to his hotel room and a five-dollar bill. He asked if I'd buy him a couple of comic books and drop them off. I used my pen to write down his room number....

2 We all become more skilled and enthusiastic writers by writing, and the more often we can encourage our adult students to write something, the better. As Moss (1998) observes, Ray Bradbury once told an audience to try and write a short story a day. Suzan-Lori Parks, the playwright and recipient of a MacArthur Fellowship "genius" award, wrote a play every day for a year (see Parks, 2006). While adults most likely will not write 55- or 100-word flash fiction stories or a play every day, the concept is an important one. If they (and you) can try their hands at writing at least one story a week, writing will become more natural and enjoyable.

3 Creating imaginative fiction continues to highlight the importance of considering adult literacy as storytelling that I discussed in Chapter 5. As Scott Russell Sanders (1997) observes, stories do many things for us as human beings. They entertain us and help build a sense of community among people. This particular lesson fosters entertainment and community building through oral and written stories, but it also promotes another quality that Sanders notes: "stories help us to see through the eyes of other people" (p. 117). And that is one of the vital aspects of literacy and literacy education.

Scary Tales and Ghost Stories

Most people enjoy a good scary story, one that makes us turn on a light or look over a shoulder. It might be one of Anne Rice's novels; classic poems like Edgar Allan Poe's "The Raven" or Robert Frost's "The Witch of Coos"; movies like *The Exorcist* or *The Sixth Sense*; or those stories we still remember from our childhood summer evenings when we tried to frighten one another (and did!) with fantastic tales about the strange man who lived down the block or the old woman who kept a butcher knife at the ready for any child who snuck into her garden. Ghost stories and short mysterious tales help adults use their imaginations in a playful and often unfettered manner. The poet William Carlos Williams commented that the value of the imagination to the writer is in its ability to make words (Williams, 1986b). And that is precisely what adult literacy education should be about—the making and celebration of words through vital reading and writing.

BEFORE THE LESSON

1 Select various ghost stories, scary tales, or weird folktales to share with your students. Try to select relatively short ones that your students can read with some ease after several shared rereadings. The flash fiction books I mentioned offer some possibilities. (There are a couple of great ones in Moss, 1998; one about a vampire and another about a werewolf.) Check with your local librarian for suggestions. I personally like to use folktale collections from different cultures. They almost all contain at least one or two strange tales of witches, ogres, beheadings, ghosts, and such. For example, in different collections of Norwegian folktales you'll find brief stories of terrifying trolls, hags who walk around with their heads under their arms, and wicked creatures always trying to capture and eat people. The Mexican tale of "La Llorona" (weeping woman), the mother who drowned her children, appears in many different versions in Mexico and the Southwestern United States. Last, Alvin Schwartz's collection of short scary stories for children (though really more appropriate for adults because of their gruesome nature), *Scary Stories to Tell in the Dark* (2006) is a book I'm never without.

2 Write a short scary story or ghost tale as a model for your students. Try to limit the number of words; 100 to 150 is a reasonable number. As an example, here's a 99-word ghost story that I've written and used as a model. I titled it "The Bar in Montana":

> The bar was empty except for the bartender and a beautiful, strangely pale woman. I ordered a beer, and the bartender grinned at me with rotten teeth.
> The woman whispered, "Join me."
> I sat across from her in the booth, but she slid next to me.
> Suddenly, she kissed me.
> It was the taste of the grave. Her tongue moved, and I struggled. She clung, but I broke free.
> She laughed hysterically through black teeth, and her tongue darted at me like a snake. I ran to the door.
> The woman and bartender shrieked, "Come back again, lover boy!"

THE LESSON, PART I

1 Ask your students if they've seen any good scary movies or television programs lately or if they know any ghost stories. Allow volunteers to share. Don't rush this story sharing time! Talk is the best kind of prewriting, and you also want to help develop a particular mood for sharing weird tales. (You might even lower the light in the room to help create the mood.)

2 Share with students the tale you selected. Read it a second time and ask students to join in. Ask for reactions. What do they think about it? What makes it weird or scary? If you have ELLs in your class, elicit from them those elements from their cultures that make something especially scary. List all ideas on chart paper.

3 Distribute copies of the tale that you've written. Read it a couple of times and ask the students to read along with you. Ask for appreciations. Describe what you were trying to do in your brief story. For example, in my ghost story I tried to take a commonplace event—walking into a bar for a drink—and turn it into a strange encounter with a dead woman. I used my first two sentences to set the mood ("strangely pale woman," bartender with "rotten teeth"), dialogue to heighten the tension, and senses to convey the horror (her kiss tasted "of the grave"). The more you can make obvious to novice writers how you go about writing the better. My experience with adults has taught me that too often they have very limited ideas about how a writer writes.

4 Ask for ideas for a scary tale or ghost story. Include any that the adults shared earlier. List them on chart paper for future use. Provide additional suggestions if necessary, for example, Faust-like stories of the devil coming for someone who sold his soul (the country song "The Devil Went Down to Georgia" by Charlie Daniels is one such popular version), the urban legend of the ghost in a white dress who hitchhikes a ride to a dance and later disappears in a graveyard (see my mother's version in Kazemek, 2002a), and so forth.

5 Ask students to take home the tales that you distributed and if possible to read them to, or with, other family members. Stress the importance of rereading. Ask them also to think about the story ideas that were brainstormed. They might also come up with others after thinking and sharing with others outside of class.

THE LESSON, PART 2

1 Begin the lesson by reading one or both of the scary stories from the previous lesson. Ask the students to read along with you. Ask for any problems the students might have had rereading the stories at home (typically certain words, phrases, or expressions; this is particularly true for ELLs). If you like you might share a new story.

2 Show the chart listing elements of scary stories and ghost stories and the chart listing possible story ideas. Ask students if they have any new ideas to add to the lists.

3 As a whole class select one of the ideas and using a modified LEA format create a short scary or ghost story of 55 to 150 words. I use the term *modified* because in this instance you should participate more in the construction of the story. You want to help the students see how a story is constructed, that is, help them incorporate dialogue, construct a strong opening sentence or "hook," create a narrative that builds with tension and suspense, and write a strong closing. Help them choose strong words. You must be careful here and proceed with tact. Typically with an LEA approach you do not offer suggestions. In this case, however, you want to help focus the students' awareness on the craft of writing. The story must be theirs, but you can encourage them to make it more interesting and specific. Here are some examples of story elements written by groups of adult students using an LEA format. I list their first openings and then their revised openings, produced with my encouragement:

> This is a strange dream. (Original)
> I do not know just how to put this on paper. (Revised)

> My family didn't believe in ghosts. (Original)
> I believe I come from a family of realists. (Revised)

> That night was black and humid. (Original)
> The air felt heavy, and the fog was thick. Leaves hung limp on the trees. (Revised)

And here are some endings:

> That was my one experience as a child in a haunted house. (Original)
> I know I was in a haunted house before I knew what the word haunted meant. (Revised)

> We never knew if it was the devil or if it was a hoax. (Original)
> "What do you think it was?" I asked my dad. "What do you think?" was his reply.
> (Revised)

4 After the class has composed a first draft, reread it with them. Emphasize the value of reconsidering word choice, revising sentences, adding dialogue, and so forth. You might use such prompts as, "What might make this scarier?" "Can you really *see* that horrible spirit sneaking into the bedroom?" and so forth.

5 Once the class has a version it likes, make copies for all members to keep in their writing folders and to reread at home and elsewhere.

6 Encourage students to try as individuals or with partners (especially in the case of ELLs) to write some additional scary or ghost stories. Suggest that students write with family members, and allot time to share the stories that are written at home, if possible. Continue to write such tales and occasionally share them with your class as models.

KEEPING ELLs IN MIND

1 This lesson continues to emphasize the use of LEA with adult students, especially ELLs. In this lesson, I described what I refer to as a teacher–student negotiated LEA process whereby the instructor takes an active role in helping to shape the particular text by modeling how a writer thinks and explores while writing. (This is similar to the think-aloud process for reading during which the instructor models how she makes meaning while reading a particular text.)

2 Telling, listening to, reading, and writing scary stories and ghost tales from their home cultures allow ELLs to use and integrate the four language modes. As Mohr (1994) observes, "ESL students benefit greatly from orally expressing their thoughts prior to writing them down. The opportunity to construct sentences in a conversational manner (listening and speaking) appears to greatly enhance the writing and associated reading process for ESL students" (p. 239).

3 The more we can build our instruction around adult ELLs' authentic experiences, language, and culture the more likely we'll be able to help them take greater expressive and creative risks in English.

WRAP UP

1 Writing about the unnatural or supernatural allows adults to expand their imaginations and create something new; it fosters imaginative control and power. As

I've been stressing throughout the book, this is precisely what adult literacy activities should do—put adults in charge of their own reading and writing. Alas, too often in workbook-based programs or workplace endeavors this does not happen. As Glynda Hull (1999) observes in one of her studies of a workplace literacy project, "It is note-worthy that workers like Marisa were expected to read and follow directions, but not to understand their significance" (p. 543).

2 Reading and writing to follow directions and to become a "functional" literate should not be the purpose of adult literacy education. Jennifer Horsman's (1990) groundbreaking work with women shows clearly that they were looking for meaning in their lives, something interesting in their days, "something to do, a social interaction and a challenge" (p. 210). However, based on deficit models, programs too often undercut the very nature of literacy. They perpetuate what Stuckey (1991) calls the "violence of literacy." Instead, literacy education should support authentic writing and reading in the adult classroom:

> Becoming a literate adult involves more than acquiring skills in reading and writing. Indeed, choosing to read and write, seeing purposeful reasons for literate behavior, and developing an ardent interest in reading and writing are at least as important as attaining basic skills. Authentic material to read and reasons to write can add an essential dimension to adult literacy programs. (Padak & Bardine, 2004, p.136)

Writing Dramatic Scripts

There has been much ado about oral reading fluency since the passage of the No Child Left Behind (NCLB) legislation, and much of it is about little (see, for example, Allington's 2005 critique). Reading quickly lists of words (often nonsense words) and passages of little value might artificially boost test scores, but it does little to improve children's comprehension, use of strategies, and love of reading. When these practices make their way into adult literacy education they become more problematic and, in-deed, potentially harmful.

Most adults with whom I have worked over the years carry emotional baggage from their early school reading experiences. Typically required to read in a "round robin" fashion, they remember their feelings of inadequacy, embarrassment, and the laughter of other children. (I have found this to be true even of undergraduate students prepar-ing to become teachers.) Moreover, almost all of the reading we do as adults is silent reading. Thus, the emphasis in adult instruction should be on developing silent reading comprehension of different texts and not on oral reading.

Nevertheless, there are times that we read orally, for example, when we read pic-ture books to our children, share something from the newspaper at the breakfast table, read instructions to another on the job, serve as a lector at a church service, and so forth. These are real purposes for oral reading, and in most cases they are reading per-formances. All oral reading in a literacy program should be of this nature—practiced performances in which adults have opportunities to become comfortable and confident with the texts they are reading. Through such meaningful practice adults will become more fluent oral readers.

Perhaps the most viable oral reading practice that I have found for use with adults as well as children and adolescents is the performance of Readers Theatre scripts. Such fun dramatic scripts allow for participation at an individual and group level and foster expressive reading. There are many scripts available, and although most are for children and adolescents some are appropriate for the adult classroom. A search on Google, for example, reveals a wealth of resources. One site that I especially like is Aaron Shepard's website (www.aaronshep.com) on which you have access to a variety of scripts based primarily on traditional tales from around the world. Many of these scripts are appropriate for adults, for example, fairy tales from the Grimm brothers, folktales from Vietnam, Iran, and other countries, and popular poetry such as Ernest Thayer's "Casey at the Bat" and Mark Twain's bitter "The War Prayer."

I have found, however, that the best scripts for adults are those that they themselves create, either from something they have read or something shaped from a piece of their own fictional or nonfictional writing. Perhaps one of the most interesting examples is the Stories of Ageing Project (1999) from Australia. A group of older women, ages 70 to 85, told the stories of their lives and then helped to shape these stories into dramatic scripts that they performed in workshops and which were captured on videotape. This was a longitudinal project that included storytelling, writing, editing, and development of theater skills. The final performed scripts focused on topics such as home, leaving home, war, work, children, food, childbirth, and mirrors. Here is the opening from the first scene of "We're Not Nice Little Old Ladies":

> Woman 1: We are not just a group of nice little old ladies you know. We are survivors, women who have experienced anguish and joy...
> Woman 2: ...success and failure...
> Woman 3: ...hope and fear...
> Woman 4: ...strength and weakness...
> Woman 1: ...and emerged, not unscathed, but more or less intact. (1999, p. 23)

This lesson highlights the writing of scripts that can later be used for Readers Theatre performances in the classroom. We will focus on transforming narratives into dramatic scripts and writing fictional scripts from scratch.

BEFORE THE LESSON

Read through the complete lesson and determine how long it might take with your group of adults. Consider any special adaptations you might have to make for your ELLs.

2 Select a Readers Theatre script that is appropriate for your group of students such as "The Calabash Kids: A Tale of Tanzania" from Aaron Shepard's website (noted previously), which begins as follows:

> Narrator 1: Once there was a woman named Shindo, who lived in a village at the foot of a snow-capped mountain.
> Narrator 4: Her husband had died, and she had no children, so she was very lonely.
> Narrator 2: And she was always tired too, for she had no one to help with the chores.
> Narrator 3: All on her own, she
> Narrator 1: cleaned the hut,
> Narrator 4: cleaned the yard,
> Narrator 2: tended the chickens,
> Narrator 3: washed her clothes in the river,
> Narrator 1: carried water,
> Narrator 4: cut firewood,
> Narrator 2: and cooked her solitary meals. (Shepard, 2002, n.p.)

3 If you cannot find a script suitable for the adults in your class, adapt one to fit your students. Read through the script a few times and determine how many readers you will need, which of your students will be best suited for which parts, and what problems might arise during the reading, for example, unusual or foreign proper nouns. Prepare copies of the script for your students by highlighting the particular speaking part on each script. For example, in the previous script I would highlight all of Narrator 1's lines for the student who would be taking that role. I'd do the same for the script I gave to the person who was reading Narrator 2's lines, and so forth. Each person must have his or her own script with the appropriate lines highlighted.

4 Compose a short fictional dramatic script as a model for your students. You might want to use something you wrote previously as a narrative and reshape it into a dramatic form. For example, here is the ghost story, "The Bar in Montana," that I wrote in the scary tales lesson, rewritten as a Readers Theatre script:

> Narrator 1: The bar was empty as the man walked inside except for the bartender and a beautiful, strangely pale woman.
> Narrator 2: He went up to the bar and ordered a beer.
> Man: I'd like a draft beer, please.
> Narrator 3: The bartender grinned at him with rotten teeth, and the pale woman approached him.
> Pale Woman: Why don't you join me?
> Narrator 1: They sat down in a booth, but the pale woman slid next to the man.
> Narrator 2: Suddenly she kissed him.
> Man: Oh, my God! Please let me go!
> Narrator 3: Her kiss tasted like the grave. The man struggled, but she clung to him.
> Man: Please, let go of me!
> Narrator 1: Finally he broke free and ran for the exit.
> Pale Woman: (Shrieking hysterically) Ha-ha-ha-ha!
> Bartender
> & Pale Woman: Come back again, lover boy!

5 Make copies of your script for the students and highlight the various parts.

THE LESSON, PART I

1 Explain to your students that together you'll be writing short pieces of fiction in the form of dramatic scripts, that is, fiction in which there is an emphasis on dialogue.

2 Ask the students to follow along as you read the script you've selected. Change your voice as you read the different parts. After you have read through the script ask for responses. Point out that this is the kind of script that movie and television actors read and memorize as they prepare for their parts.

3 Assign different parts to your students. Depending on the number of adults in your class and their reading abilities, you might have two or three individuals take one character or narrator part. Match ELLs with native English speakers. Have the students rehearse their parts a couple of times. Circulate and assist where needed. Be sure to take one of the parts yourself (usually with one of the less proficient readers or one of the ELLs).

4 Read the script as a whole class with individuals or partners reading their parts. Then discuss the importance of performing the script, that is, using dramatic intonation, pacing, and so forth. I usually suggest that we "read it like movie stars would." Read or perform the script a second time.

5 Usually introducing, reading, rehearsing, and performing a short Readers Theatre script is plenty for a first attempt.

THE LESSON, PART 2

1 Begin by reviewing what you did during the last meeting. If adults are eager, perform the script again.

2 Distribute copies of the Readers Theatre script you wrote. If you simply transformed a narrative into a dramatic script (as I did), explain the transformation. This helps to make obvious what you did as a writer. Read the script and have the adults follow along.

3 Suggest that you write a fictional Readers Theatre script as a whole class. You have several options here. If the class has already written a scary tale or ghost story from the previous lesson, together you can modify it into a dramatic script. If you have a group of students who are especially social and comfortable with one another, you can try a simple "story around," that is, you begin a story, for example, "I was driving past a graveyard last night, and I heard someone call out, 'Come here!'" Then ask for someone to add the next line, for example, "It was a woman in white, and she said, 'I need your help.'" This kind of "storying around" naturally highlights dialogue. Your third option is to brainstorm as a whole class for ideas, characters, dialogue, and so forth with you listing the items on the dry-erase board or chart paper.

4 Using an LEA format, help the class write a short Readers Theatre script. Unlike in most other LEA activities, you might want to take the more active teacher–student negotiated LEA role that I described in the previous lesson. For example, you might want to suggest that there be more than one narrator, more dialogue, additional characters, and so on. You want to help the students understand better the nature of a dramatic piece of writing. Try to get a first draft of a complete script during this meeting.

5 Ask students to think about the script they have written before the next meeting. Ask them to consider anything they might add to make it more dramatic.

6 Before the next meeting make copies of the first draft for all students.

THE LESSON, PART 3

1 Distribute copies of the first draft. Read through it and ask the students to follow along.

2 Ask for any new ideas that might make the script stronger or more interesting. Add them and make any changes the students suggest.

3 As a whole class, read through the entire script. Again ask if they'd like to make any changes.

4 Have the adults select parts, or assign them if necessary. Have individuals or partners rehearse and then perform the script. If students are comfortable with being videotaped and if you have access to a video camera, suggest that you'll bring in copies of the final script for the next meeting and videotape the performance.

5 Here's the start of a script from one group of adults. Some of the ideas came from the 55-word stories we had been reading:

Narrator 1: The mother was out looking for her daughter.
Narrator 2: She was not very happy.
Mother: She's going to get it when I catch her.
Narrator 3: The mother saw a scantily clad young woman hitchhiking on the side of the road.
Daughter: Oh, oh, I'm in trouble now!

6 Encourage students to try to compose their own short scripts at home. If your students especially enjoy performing dramatic scripts, you might want to explore some of the very short plays in Suzan-Lori Parks's *365 Days/365 Plays* (2006).

KEEPING ELLs IN MIND

1 Readers Theatre scripts are especially valuable for your ELLs because they foster interesting and enjoyable opportunities to try out spoken English. Moreover, ELLs can see the connections among reading, writing, speaking, and listening when an LEA approach is used. Last, because the student-composed scripts are typically short, parts can be highlighted for even those adults with limited English abilities, for example, "She was not very happy" in the student script example. Everyone can participate.

2 Writing and performing Readers Theatre scripts can be meaningfully connected to simple poetry and repetitive songs and chants that allow ELLs to practice spoken English by taking different parts. Moreover, particular aspects of language can be emphasized through such activities, for example, past, present, and future tenses; declarative, exclamatory, and interrogative sentence structures, and so on. I have found Carolyn Graham's *Jazz Chants: Rhythms of American English for Students of English as a Second Language* (1978) to be most beneficial and fun for ELLs as well as native English speakers. Many of the chants are already arranged into two speaking parts. "Major Decisions" begins,

> How do you like your coffee?
> Black! Black!
> How do you like your tea?
> With lemon, please? (p. 39)

Jazz Chants and several follow-up books by Graham all come with audiotapes that provide models of spoken English for you and your students.

WRAP UP

1 A group of elder writers with whom I have worked for more than 10 years now (Kazemek, 1999) enjoys writing Readers Theatre scripts of various kinds and performing them for and often with elementary children. They call themselves "The Story Readers." Adults in your class who have children at home can do the same thing with their own children.

2 In the Newfoundland fishing community that William Fagan (1998) studied, television, radio talk shows, song, and drama were regular experiences of the people there.

> While drama was always played out via oral language, at times when "a play was made up" it may have been written down to foster the ease of memorization for the actors; however, it was not uncommon to "sketch out" the sequence of a play, memorize this, and then choose the appropriate language, which may undergo slight variations each time the play was rehearsed or staged. (p. 169)

This, it seems to me, is as good a summary of this lesson as any.

CHAPTER 7

Making It Better: Working With the Mechanics of Texts

HOW DO WE help adults become more sophisticated and skillful in improving their writing in terms of content as well as such conventions as grammar and punctuation? Over the last couple of decades I've discovered that most adults with whom I've worked want their writing to be "correct." They are very concerned with form, sometimes to the detriment of the content. At one time I dismissed or downplayed their concerns about correctness. I'd say something like, "Don't worry about punctuation, spelling, and such; it's your story or poem that counts." Usually they would humor me and appear to agree with my comments. I guess I'm a slow learner, but it took me some time to recognize the serious expressions on their faces as indicators of the trouble they had with my blithe remarks.

One day while we were sharing brief stories that we had written a student sitting next to me commented, "You know, Frank, yours is always so clean, you know, the printing, spelling, and punctuation." She was looking at my printed double-spaced, edited, and spell-checked story and comparing it to her handwritten one with several misspellings. I suddenly realized that of course we all want to get it "correct." I strive for such correctness in my own personal and professional writing, making a special effort before I submit something to a magazine or journal. Why shouldn't adult literacy students, even those with the most basic skills, want their writing to be just as good in terms of mechanics?

In this chapter I want to explore with you some principles and strategies for helping adult writers "get it right" without reaffirming mistaken notions they might have about writing and without interfering with their imaginative explorations of language and creative expressions of self. I still stand by the general strategies that my colleague Pat Rigg and I stated more than a decade ago (Kazemek & Rigg, 1995, p. 85):

- Model for students by oral reading
- Use material that encourages prediction
- Foster a sense of community within the class
- Value individual interpretation

- Provide various kinds of structure for students' writing
- Support and guide students' risk taking
- Participate in all the reading and writing activities

All of the lessons in the preceding chapters have been based to some degree or another upon these general strategies.

In the following pages I present some specific ideas for helping adults make their writing better and for expanding their understanding of different language forms and elements. All of these ideas can be modified and incorporated as needed into any of the lessons in this book as integral parts or as stand-alone minilessons. Specifically, I explore revision, vocabulary development, spelling, and grammar and punctuation.

As noted in the Introduction, this chapter differs from the preceding six. Instead of detailed lesson plans, I present a number of *activities* that can be used to help adults become more skillful in their writing with such things as revision, vocabulary use, spelling, punctuation, and grammar. These activities are designed for use with adults only as needed; they are *not* to be used in any sequence or to be rigidly followed. They reflect what I have encountered and learned over the years while writing with adults of all ages and students of all ages. Hopefully, they will help you look closely at what your students are doing and then serve as catalysts for generating your own specific activities. Finally, I make no distinction between native English speakers and ELLs in this chapter. The activities can be easily modified to work with all students.

Revision—Looking Again at a First Draft

In her study of six American women whose literacy had been "shut down" in one way or another, Daphne Key (1998) describes what one of the women, Beverly, a 60-year-old college graduate, remembered about writing in school: "mechanics and books on how to write papers" (p. 53). Accordingly, although Beverly feels that writing is a means of expression, she still believes that "writing is dictated by what is perceived to be correct, as are speaking and reading" (p. 53). And, more important, Beverly's beliefs result in her self-admitted shutting down of other people, for example friends, in terms of "correctness," of spoken as well as written language. Thus, it is vital that as literacy educators we are alert to our own past experiences and biases when we begin to help adult students work with and revise their writing. It is too easy (as I know from my own teaching mistakes) to unconsciously convey a mistaken notion of correctness and contribute to the shutting down of individuals' literacy.

Revision is a difficult process, regardless of what all the composition books maintain. Sometimes a person simply likes what she has written in a first draft and feels no need to change anything. Suggestions from the instructor or some sort of peer sharing group will distract or "shut down" the writer. Sometimes the person simply doesn't know how to make the writing better; this is often the case with ELLs who possess limited English. Moreover, every piece of writing does not have to go beyond a first draft; this is especially true with adults who are just beginning to gain confidence as writers. My main point here is that input from the instructor or peers can be valuable to an individual writer, but suggestions and invitations to revise must be done with skill and tact. We want adult literacy students to feel the flow of writing. With these concerns in mind, here are some strategies that I have found to be helpful with adult writers.

CAN I TAKE ANYTHING OUT?

Less is usually more when it comes to writing. Most of us intentionally or unintentionally pad our writing. I have found this to be true even with less skilled writers. Using your own writing as models you can show students how you have taken out words, phrases, or sentences to make the piece stronger. For example, here's a first draft sentence from a short story and then the revised version that I shared with students:

> She shuddered spasmodically when she saw the horned owl perched lightly on a rafter. (First draft)
> She shuddered when she saw the horned owl perched on a rafter. (Revised)

After exploring with students why you made particular choices and discussing their perspectives on your decisions, have them do the same thing with a piece of their own writing that they want to make stronger. This often works best with a partner, especially with an ELL and native English speaker team. At first you might instruct them to take out only one word. Here are a couple of student examples. The first highlights the difference between spoken and written language. Instead of using "and" as a connector, the writer shifts to the punctuation of a written text.

> She walked to the front of the room and put down her bag and quickly counted heads and said, "Good morning." (First draft)
> She walked to the front of the room, put down her bag, quickly counted heads, and said, "Good morning." (Revised)

Here's an example where a student realized he was overusing repetition:

> She hollered and hollered like crazy at me, "Get away from here!" (First draft)
> She hollered at me, "Get away from here!" (Revised)

The more you get students to look at your writing and their own in terms of what might be left out, the more comfortable they will become with this simple form of revision. Whole-class minilessons, partner work, and individual revisions are more options for this activity.

CAN I ADD ANYTHING (WORD, PHRASE, OR SENTENCE) THAT HELPS ME PAINT A MORE VIVID PICTURE?

This strategy is typically known as "sentence expansion," and it is useful for helping adults explore and expand the world of language. Victoria Purcell-Gates in her instructive and important study *Other People's Words: The Cycle of Low Literacy* (1995) observes,

> Literacy opens up a world of language to readers not available in a purely oral culture. Written language employs more varied vocabulary and a level of vocabulary that can be described as "literary" or "written." Words like *employ, participate*, and *acquisition* are more likely to appear in print than in one's conversation, where they would likely be replaced by *use, join in,* and *learn* or *get*.... (p. 166)

Use your own writing as examples to explore with students how you made various additions to improve the piece of poetry or prose. Minilessons on the use of a basic thesaurus, dictionary, or language/thesaurus tool (if students have access to computers and word processing programs) are useful here. Such reference tools should only be used in conjunction with students' own writing. Here are a few student examples with the additions shown in the second sentence:

> She always wore clothing as if she was cold all the time. (Original)
> She always wore several layers of clothing as if she was cold all the time. (Revised)

> She also had a couple of her toes cut off. (Original)
> She also had a couple of her toes amputated. (Revised)

> I would exchange my soul/For one that shuns the goal. (Original)
> I would exchange my passionate soul/For one that shuns the impossible goal. (Revised)

Encouraging students to expand their writing through the use of reference books, discussion, questioning, and "lifting" of vocabulary they like from other texts is not only important for native English speakers but more so for ELLs with limited oral and written English vocabulary.

CAN I USE THE REPORTER'S 5Ws & H (WHO, WHAT, WHERE, WHEN, WHY, & HOW) TO CREATE A MORE COMPLETE PIECE?

In various lessons (for example, on prose vignettes) we've already explored ways of using the 5Ws & H as a means of organizing or structuring a piece of writing. These questions can also be used during revision to make the piece more complete and "reader friendly." This is especially useful with prose writing. Here's an example of mine that I often use with students. It is a work of flash fiction under 100 words. First is the original then the revised version:

> We lost Ozzie in Grandpa's oak tree. We had been playing "higher-than-the-ground" when the stars started twinkling in the sky. Ozzie had been "it" for most of the game.

He was never able to get himself up on, say, a car fender before being tagged and made "it." As dark closed in he managed somehow to work himself up into the great oak. He became disoriented in the branches, and it was three days before his father finally found him. (Original)

We lost my cousin Ozzie in Grandpa's oak tree. We had been playing "higher-than-the-ground" when the stars started twinkling in the south side Chicago sky. Ozzie had been "it" for most of the game because of his weight and awkwardness. He was never fast enough to catch others or agile enough to get himself up on, say, a car fender before being tagged and made "it." As dark closed in he managed somehow to work himself up into the great oak. He became disoriented in the branches, and it was three days before his father finally found him. (Revised)

Notice in the second version I clarify Who, Where, and Why.

Again, specific minilessons work here, but also try to get students to think about the 5Ws & H *while* they are in the process of drafting. Stress that writing isn't simply a linear, step-by-step process, but instead is a recursive one in which the "steps" overlap.

CAN I USE ANY OF THE FIVE SENSES (SEEING, HEARING, TASTING, SMELLING, OR FEELING) TO PAINT A "RICHER" PICTURE?

Mark Twain (1888) once observed that the difference between the right word and the almost right word is the difference between lightning and a lightning bug. This is especially true with poetry and its emphasis on particulars. Because most poetry that adult literacy students (and most of us) write is relatively short, this is a good place to look closely at word choice during revision. A single word change can help make a poem stronger.

Obviously, with poetry we're dealing with figurative language. When we're revising by asking what it looks, sounds, tastes, smells, or feels like we're working with similes and metaphors. We don't want to use the terms *similes* and *metaphors*, however, because as I've once written, talking about "figurative language will not only get in the way of the poetry but may bring back unpleasant school memories for some adults" (Kazemek & Rigg, 1995, p. 11). Instead, we merely want adults to look again at their poems to see if a different word or words will make it richer and livelier.

Again it's best to show examples from your own writing and then to encourage adults to look closely and try alternatives with their own. Here is one of my poems as an example. The first poem is the original, and the second is the revised version:

> The flowering crabapple
> knows nothing of Vivaldi,
> but its myriad notes
> blossoming on branches
> play music more
> lovely than his "Spring." (Original)

> The flowering crabapple
> knows nothing of Vivaldi,
> but its myriad notes
> blossoming on the bars
> of branches play a music
> more lovely than his "Spring." (Revised)

I explain to students that I was thinking of the bar lines, or measures, on a musical score as I was revising this poem. I saw the flowers as single and double bar lines on the branches. (I also tell them that I liked the /b/ sound in *blossoming, bars,* and *branches*.)

Here are a few examples from students' poetry.

> Our little yacht felt
> Like a rowboat afloat
> In a giant ocean. (Original)

> Our little yacht felt
> Like an eggshell afloat
> In a giant ocean. (Revised)

> Fruit juice skin
> The beauty in life
> Of oranges (Original)

> Fruit juice skin
> The taste in life
> Of oranges (Revised)

> Winter fun
> Playing tag together
> And the moon
> On the frozen creek (Original)

> Winter fun
> Playing tag together
> Evening lit with lanterns
> And the moon
> On the frozen creek (Revised)

The more we can get adults to think and talk about word choices, images, and the particulars of language and writing, the more subtle and adept they will become with print. Such thinking, talking, and revising in the community of a supportive classroom will free them to explore in a way that most have not been able to in their earlier school years.

CAN I HEAR THE WAY IT SOUNDS? CAN IT SOUND BETTER?

The writer Eudora Welty (1984) observes,

Ever since I was first read to, then started reading to myself, there has never been a line read that I didn't *hear*. As my eyes followed the sentence, a voice was saying it silently to me. It isn't my mother's voice, or the voice of any person I can identify, certainly not my own. It is human, but inward, and it is inwardly that I listen to it. It is to me the voice of the story or poem itself. The cadence, whatever it is that asks you to believe, the feeling resides in the printed word, reaches me through the reader-voice. (pp. 11–12)

Adults with limited reading skills, whether native speakers or ELLs, cannot hear, or have a difficult time hearing, that reader-voice. That's why I've stressed throughout the book the importance of model reading by the teacher and the repeated choral reading by students in a safe context. We want them to move beyond the decoding of individual words and into the flow of language.

We can also use oral reading as a revision strategy. Simply by reading back to a writer in a careful and considerate manner his draft of a poem or piece of prose, we can help him hear where things might need to be changed. I know that many people suggest writers reading aloud their own work, and I think that is useful in limited circumstances. However, it's hearing a fluent and enthusiastic reader read our work that best helps us see its strengths, weaknesses, and potential. This is especially true for writers in adult literacy classes.

Vocabulary Development—Choosing the Best Word

How do we help adults expand their reading and writing vocabularies? Through the various packaged programs, kits, and workbooks that are so readily available? Obviously not. As I've emphasized throughout the book, we develop our "word hoards" through repeated purposeful encounters and use. Stephen Krashen (2004) has summarized decades of research that shows Free Voluntary Reading (FVR) improves children's reading, writing, spelling, and vocabulary. From my experience, the same applies to adults. When they are encountering the same words again and again in their own self-selected reading and using many of those words in their own writing, then their reading and writing vocabularies expand.

William Nagy's (1988) important research into vocabulary development and instruction highlights the "three properties essential to powerful vocabulary instruction—integration, repetition, and meaningful use" (p. 31). Based on these properties, here are some activities that over the years I have found to be helpful.

SHARED READING AND REREADING

Oral reading and rereading of high-interest texts—published stories and poems, students' writing, children's picture books, and other texts such as magazines, newspaper articles, fliers, and so on—with you as a model is a natural way to demonstrate good oral reading and to expose students to a wide range of vocabulary. By modeling first while students follow along silently and then having the whole class reread aloud while you provide assisted reading support if needed, the students have safe opportunities to try out a wide range of vocabulary. They can then reread texts of interest in small groups or partner pairings. Rereading is especially important for ELLs.

SELF-SELECTED READING

Adults should have opportunities during each class meeting to read silently something they have chosen. Again, it might be pieces of their own writing, writing of other students that you've collected into booklets, published stories, poems, children's books, magazines, and so forth. Adults need to engage in literate behavior if they are to become more literate, and silent reading is one of the things most literate people do. Victoria Purcell-Gates (1995) contends (and I agree strongly) that "the most effective 'reading instruction' is composed for the most part of encouraging and facilitating volume reading by the learner for personally meaningful reasons" (p. 132).

KEEPING WORD BANKS OR WORD CACHES

Students can keep cards of vocabulary they like, find interesting, or need from whole-group texts created using an LEA format, their own writing, and from their reading. Particularly relevant here are words that adults encounter and use in their everyday informal literacy practices, whether at home, in the community, or on the job (Taylor, 2006). These cards (typically index cards collected in a box) can then be used for further writing, a review of "sight words," and for specific instruction in phonics and spelling. An added value of keeping word banks or caches is that they give adults a *quantitative* psychological boost to their expanding literacy. You'll hear such comments as, "Man, Frank, look at all of the cards I have in my bank. I know a lot of words!"

TEACHING SKILLS LESSONS

Research (for example, Purcell-Gates et al., 2002) has shown that there need not be a divide between skills instruction and adult literacy practices *as long as both the instruction and practices are authentic and purposeful to the students*. We can (and should) help adults develop their ability to decode new or unfamiliar words by using the context in which they appear and phonics instruction. This does *not* mean the use of workbook pages or "canned" phonics programs on the computer. Instead, it means using the adults' own reading and writing as the basis for specific—and needed—lessons. What native English speakers of differing ability and ELLs need in terms of instruction and practice with sound–symbol correspondence, for example, will always vary dramatically. To use the cliché, one size does not fit all. As an example, here's the poem written using an LEA format from the lesson on bio-poems:

> I seem to be a talker/but I'm really a listener
> I seem to be yesterday/but I'm really tomorrow

I seem to be a grape/but I'm really a vine
I seem to be a honeybee/but I'm really a cricket
I seem to be a lake/but I'm really a creek

A little poem like this offers many possibilities for specific instruction: letter–sound correspondence (*s, t, b, r, l*), consonant blends (*cr, gr*), vowel digraphs (*ee, ea*), silent-*e* long vowel sound (*grape, lake*), rimes (*-ut, -ine, -eek*), compound words (*honeybee*), and simple and compound sentences. The key thing here is that the particular adult actually needs a lesson on a particular skill. More important, however, is our responsibility to help adults—to teach them—with those aspects of reading and writing that are unfamiliar to them. As Purcell-Gates (1995) insists,

> Reading and writing are cultural practices, and direct instruction is required for those experiencing problems with them. It is unfair and unethical to withhold insider information until children, or adults, "figure it out for themselves," as if they were insiders all along. (p. 98)

Spelling—Wrestling With English Orthography

Spelling is often the bane of adults who have not been successful in school and are convinced that if they can't spell correctly they won't be able to read and write "correctly." Such mistaken notions usually get in the way of writing, and we as educators often find it difficult to help our adult students think otherwise. Spelling is a tool that serves writing, but we can't be dismissive of our students' real or exaggerated concerns about correctness. We should respect those concerns and work with them by offering support and strategies. Following are strategies that I have found to be useful at different times with different people.

PUT SPELLING IN CONTEXT

A brief discussion and demonstration of how the English language and spelling have changed over the centuries is useful in showing adults *why* English spelling is not regular. Such a lesson also is valuable for ELLs whose native language (for instance, Spanish) is highly regular. English is a conglomeration of various root sources (it's a member of the Indo-European family of languages) along with countless words from other languages. Moreover, we continue to add new words daily. Thus, showing examples from Old English (*Beowulf* works here), Middle English (try Chaucer's *Canterbury Tales*), Elizabethan English (use Shakespeare), and examples of Modern English variants (*labor* in American English but *labour* in British and Canadian English) will help students get a better understanding of why it's often hard to spell words correctly. Such an overview will also help adults see that their commonsense (and widely used commercial) spellings of such words as *lite* and *rite* instead of *light* and *right* do indeed make sense! Such lessons and discussions are sadly missing from many literacy programs. There seems to be an underlying assumption that adults don't care about such things or that they aren't relevant to the teaching of "basic skills."

MODEL SPELLING

In the past I stressed the importance of having adults experiment with their spellings: "The more you can encourage risk taking and language play among your students the better. When your students are writing the first draft of a poem, you want them to concentrate on creating the poem" (Kazemek & Rigg, 1995, p. 89). Well, yes, and no. We do indeed want adults to play and take risks with their spellings; "invented" or "place holding" spelling is vital. However, over the ensuing years I've discovered that it's more complex than that. Some adults *want* the correct spelling as they're writing a first draft and not having it gets in the way of their creation of the poem or other text. Moreover, Victoria Purcell-Gates (1995) observes quite rightly that beginning readers

> should not repeatedly "read" unconventional spellings and punctuation. This practice will nei-
> ther aid their automatic recognition of words nor help them begin to gain an intuitive feel for
> conventional spelling patterns or written punctuation conventions. This does not mean that
> encouraging invented spelling is wrong; many good theoretical reasons exist for this practice....
> Rather, the "published" writing read by those learning to read and write needs to be in conven-
> tional form to provide the "convention" toward which the learner is moving." (p. 132)

And conventional patterns are even more important for ELLs who are trying to figure out the language.

What's to be done? I still advocate the use of invented spelling while adults are working on first drafts. However, I now always have in hand a packet of sticky notes. If an individual is writing and asks me how a word is spelled, I no longer say, "Give it a go, and don't worry." I'll simply write the word on a sticky note and give it to her. (If I'm not sure about the correct spelling, I'll write the word and put a question mark after it, for example, "occassion?") If she chooses she can later add the word to her spelling folder. (See next section.) ELLs especially benefit from the sticky note strategy. This modeling strategy supports the risk taking of those adults who are comfortable with "giving it a go" on first drafts and the needs of those adults who are less linguistically adventurous or for whom English is not their native language.

USE PERSONAL SPELLING FOLDERS

A personal spelling folder or dictionary is a useful tool for many adults. In it they can keep an alphabetized list of words that *they* want to spell correctly. These words can come from their own writing, reading, or from lists of typically misspelled words. Words from word banks or word caches (described previously) might also be included in the folder. Such folders are particularly beneficial for ELLs. The important thing is that students use their folders. If they simply add words but never go back to their folders while writing or after writing to check spellings, then the folders are of little value and simply another "school exercise." Encourage adults to keep folders or dictionaries only if they find them useful. Don't make it a practice for all students.

TEACH SELECTED MINILESSONS

English spelling is sometimes confusing, but there are some predictable and useful generalizations that we can teach adults in short minilessons. Some obvious ones include the following: *ei* and *ie* ("*i* before *e* except after *c*" *does* work most of the time), *y* to *i* and add *es*, double consonants before suffixes (for example, *run, running*), *w* always silent before *r* (*wrap, write*), *k* always silent before *n* (*known*), consonant-vowel-consonant-*e* (*save, plane*). Onsets and rimes (word families) are valuable because once an adult knows the rime, she can use that knowledge to spell other words in the word family, for example, *-ate* gives one spelling access to *crate, date, mate, plate, state, inflate, debate, rebate*, and so forth. Highlighting common homophones that are often confused can be of help to many adult writers (it would help some of my undergraduate students as well!), for example, *right, write, their, there, they're, whole, hole, your, you're, to, too, two, close, clothes*, and so forth. Such minilessons should be based on the specific needs of adults; we shouldn't teach them simply because they are part of some skills program or book.

ANALYZE ADULTS' MISSPELLINGS

In order to plan and develop minilessons it is especially useful to look closely at the kinds of misspellings adults are making. Generally, these misspellings will fall in various groups. For example, *libary* for *library* and *yellin* for *yelling* reflect a common spoken form of these words; dialect differences and the influence of a person's native, non-English language will also affect spelling. The use of the wrong vowel (*obay* for *obey*), omission (*lisen* for *listen*), consonant confusion (*chozen* for *chosen*), and so on will give you the specific content of your minilessons. Robin Millar (2007) points out that you can analyze spelling errors according to five categories:

1. Spell word like it sounds ("dum" for "dumb")
2. Rule or generalization problem ("Steela" for "Stella")
3. Letters out of order ("frist" for "first")
4. Sounds mixed up or omitted ("souned" for "sounded")
5. Significant parts missing ("listen" for "listened")

Thus, through analysis of errors you can help adults see that spelling is more than "sounding out" words. It "requires knowledge of phonics, word patterns, syllabication, and spelling rules" (Millar, 2007, pp. 84–85). Through such exploration you can build spelling lessons around what adults are actually doing in their writing.

PROMOTE THE USE OF SPELL-CHECKERS AND SPELLING HANDBOOKS

Spelling is an individual skill and accomplishment. Some people are simply better spellers than others are. (Remember those who always won the spelling bee with little effort in elementary school?) I know very smart people with advanced degrees who are terrible spellers. Thus, we should always encourage standard spelling in final drafts because we want adults' work to be as good as possible; however, we should not make spelling as important as writing and reading themselves. Marshall McLuhan (1994) says that all technology is an extension of the human mind and hand. Accordingly, we should promote the use of such technologies as spell-checkers on computers, the kinds of little spelling handbooks that secretaries sometimes still use, and the adults' own individual spelling folders. Ultimately, we want adults to realize that they do not need to know how to spell correctly all the words that they write and read. No one is able to do that. What's important is knowing where to find the correct spelling with as little effort as possible.

Grammar and Punctuation—Deciding Between Spoken and Written Language

I have been writing with students from ages 8 to 88 for almost three decades now, and for that period of time I've seen basically the same grammar and punctuation errors in their writing. My college students sometimes still write "The *person* forgot *their* book," or "If an *individual* waits long enough, *they* will get a seat." Sentence fragments abound at all levels, elementary through university and adult education: "The girl wanted out of the city. A dangerous place." Similarly, the ability to discern independent and dependent clauses is sometimes lacking or misunderstood: "Sandy was a smart dog we decided to teach her tricks." "I was in a Goodwill truck on a big hill and this lady got stuck." "Her son, we were arguing over some hamburger meat and she said she didn't know us." Of course, because of linguistic insecurity we hear daily on television and radio the misuse of "I" and "me" from pundits, politicians, and people from all walks of life: "It was a real struggle between him and I." "Gloria and me decided to break up."

What accounts for these mistakes on the part of people with 12 to 16 years of education? I think that research over the decades with beginning and nonproficient writers shows us that writers write the way they talk, that is, their writing reflects the informal registers of their spoken language. This is especially true with adult literacy students. And this is often compounded when well-meaning educators tell adult students that "writing is just talk written down." Well, it's not. As the Russian psychologist, Lev Vygotsky (1978) says, writing is a second order symbolism. Thus, when an instructor simply transcribes adults' LEA texts and subsequently never *uses* them to highlight the differences between talk and more formal writing, she leads her students down a narrow road of restricted choices.

James Paul Gee's (2008) discussion of Discourses is relevant here. A Discourse (with a capital *D*), he says, "is a socially accepted association among ways of using language and other symbolic expressions, of thinking, feeling, believing, valuing, and act-ing...that can be used to identify oneself as a member of a socially meaningful group or 'social network'..." (p.161). All adult literacy students bring their primary Discourses to the classroom with the intent of acquiring secondary Discourses, that is, various forms of literacy, through language "acquisition" and "learning." (See my references to Stephen Krashen's 1982 discussion of these terms throughout the book.) While the lessons in this book highlight "acquisition," that is, becoming more fluent writers and readers by playing around with various kinds of writing and exploring different models in supportive social contexts, I am not discounting "learning," that is, the conscious knowledge gained through specific teaching, analysis, and reflection.

Gee (2008) contends that the Acquisition Principle and Learning Principle are *both* important. "Teaching that leads to acquisition means to apprentice students in a master–apprentice relationship in a Discourse wherein the teacher scaffolds the stu-dents' growing abilities...." (p. 178). Teaching for learning, on the other hand, "uses ex-planations and analyses that break down material into its analytic 'bits' and...develops 'meta-knowledge'" (p. 178). Gee argues that meta-knowledge can be a form of power and liberation. He concludes, "Teaching for acquisition alone leads to successful but 'colonized' students. Teaching for acquisition and teaching for learning are different practices, and good teachers do both" (p. 178).

Accordingly, discussions of and minilessons on grammar and punctuation should be opportunities to explore a number of different linguistic roads, most of them applicable in different contexts and for different purposes. Sometimes we want to capture spoken language in writing and we will use informal or nonstandard grammar: "'I ain't got none,' he said." "He be goin' to the store." We don't worry about grammar and punctuation when we're writing a note to leave on the refrigerator. However, at other times we might want to use more Standard English in a note, for example, in a brief letter to a child's teacher. The key, I believe, is to help adult students see that grammar and punc-tuation are more than the worksheets and rules that all too many of them struggled with during their school days. Instead we want them to see that there are variations of language use, and that these can be explored in their own reading and writing. Following are some strategies that I have found useful in my own work.

TEACH MINILESSONS ON SENTENCE EXPANSION

Engaging your students in sentence expansion activities helps them see not only how they might make their writing more specific but also how they might use punctuation. I typically use examples from published texts and (when an individual volunteers his own work) from students' writing. Of course, I use authors I love. Here's a typical example from Ernest Hemingway's short story "Big Two-Hearted River Part I" (Hemingway, 1987, p. 163) and the way one group of students expanded it:

Nick looked down into the pool from the bridge. It was a hot day. A kingfisher flew up the stream. (Original)
Nick looked down into the deep pool from the old, wooden bridge. It was a hot, stuffy day. A large, beautiful kingfisher flew up from the sparkling stream. (Revised)

Here's an example from a student's writing and then its expanded version:

Sandy had two litters. The puppies were cute. (Original)
Sandy had two large litters. The squirming, bouncing, barking puppies were yellow, big-eared, and cute. (Revised)

I have found that sentence expansion lessons work best in group settings. The interaction, suggestions, and questions generated by students usually help to clarify concepts.

TEACH MINILESSONS ON SENTENCE COMBINING

Sentence combining is perhaps the best strategy for helping adults see that writing involves making stylistic choices, and that punctuation allows us to say the same thing in slightly different ways. Once again, I use examples from authors I admire and from students' own work. Here's the Hemingway passage and how I and a group of students combined the sentences:

Nick looked down into the pool from the bridge. It was a hot day. A kingfisher flew up the stream. (Original)

Multiple revisions

Nick looked down into the pool from the bridge, and it was a hot day. A kingfisher flew up the stream.

Nick looked down into the pool from the bridge on a hot day, and a kingfisher flew up the stream.

Nick looked down into the pool from the bridge. It was a hot day, and a kingfisher flew up the stream.

Nick looked down into the pool from the bridge on a hot day; a kingfisher flew up the stream.

Here's a student example and then the way the whole group combined her sentences:

The girl sat under the tree. A bird sang. (Original)

Multiple revisions

The girl sat under the tree, and a bird sang.

The girl sat under the tree; a bird sang.

The girl sat under the tree while a bird sang.

Sentence combining helps your students come to a greater realization and use of print conventions and helps them become more sophisticated in constructing texts.

ENCOURAGE STUDENTS TO IMITATE DIFFERENT MODELS

I have stressed throughout this book the importance of modeling, by the teacher as well as by the use of various kinds of texts chosen as catalysts for students' reading and writing. Such modeling also works in an immediate way by having students imitate or "shadow" a piece of writing that is well written. The writing might be prose or poetry. Encouraging students as individuals or partners (especially ELLs with native English speakers) to imitate a piece of writing and then exploring the student versions as a whole class for correctness offers a wealth of opportunities for examining punctuation and grammar. Following is another passage from Hemingway's "Big Two-Hearted River Part I" (1987) and then an imitated version written by a small group of adults:

Original Version
He started a fire with some chunks of pine he got with the ax from a stump. Over the fire he stuck a wire grill, pushing the four legs down into the ground with his boot. Nick put the frying pan on the grill over the flames. He was hungrier. The beans and spaghetti warmed. Nick stirred them and mixed them together. They began to bubble, making little bubbles that rose with difficulty to the surface. There was a good smell. (pp. 167–168)

Imitated Version
She started her bread with some flour and yeast she got from the cabinet. Inside a bowl she poured some water, mixing the yeast into it. Irene mixed the flour into the bowl with a spoon. She was busier. The flour and yeast worked. Irene punched them and folded them together. They began to rise, making a smell that filled the kitchen. There was a sweet smell.

In our exploration of Hemingway's piece and the one that we wrote together, we were able to explore such things as complete sentences, prepositional phrases, use of punctuation, and a particular style of writing.

Similarly, I have used different lines and passages from poetry for this activity. I try to use poets whose work is superior and provides clean examples to imitate, for example, Robert Frost (1969):

Original Version
Some say the world will end in fire,
Some say in ice. (p. 220)

And the students' version:

Some say the spring will end in rain,
Some say in snow.

PLAY WITH PUNCTUATION AND PARTS OF SPEECH

Almost all of the adult literacy students (and most of the university students too) with whom I've worked have negative memories of grammar instruction from their school days. It was dreary, spirit-deadening stuff—worksheets, circling and underlining words, and sweating over phrases and sentences that meant little. Thus, if you're going to explore grammar with your students (and many adults *do* want to have some competency in being able to identify a verb, adjective, and so on), then the best thing you can do is to have them play around with the language. I have found several books and resources to be useful. Of course, *The Elements of Style* (Strunk & White, 1979) is still a touchstone of many writers and teachers, and it is one I still refer to at times. Karen Elizabeth Gordon's *The Transitive Vampire: A Handbook of Grammar for the Innocent, the Eager, and the Doomed* (1984) and the updated edition *The Deluxe Transitive Vampire: The Ultimate Handbook of Grammar for the Innocent, the Eager, and the Doomed* (1993) offer wonderfully humorous and engaging examples to read, laugh at, and use in one's own writing. An example for "Verb" is "I *fancy* dames with broad shoulders." An "Adjective" example is "Her *fancy* dress showed them off to great advantage." And a "Noun" example is "I therefore took a *fancy* to her" (Gordon, 1984, p. 9). I've used many of her examples and those from other sources to have students play around with multiple-meaning words and homophones. Such play is also valuable for ELLs, especially if done in group settings. For example, playing with grammar in various game formats allows even those adults with limited English abilities to become actively involved: "In my class, students experimented with possible word combinations, discussing their choices aloud, coaching each other, and sharing their collective knowledge" (Coustan, 2004, p. 89). Such play can help you avoid putting students inadvertently on the defensive, and thus, can help lower students' concern over making errors (Krashen, 1982).

Writing silly sentences or little nonsense stories is both fun and valuable for helping adults learn how to use different vocabulary and parts of speech in their writing. Following are some homophone examples written by different students over the years:

I was bored with the washing board.

I knew she had a new boyfriend.

He threw the ball through the window.

And here are examples of two stories written by ELL and native English speaker teams:

Give two dollars to that man to buy some beer. By the way, he's too loaded to buy it himself.

They're going to leave their children at home while they go out for supper. There will be a lot of mischief while they're gone.

Mad Libs of all sorts in inexpensive tablets are available in bookstores, gift shops, and party stores. They have been around a long time and have been played in many settings. Each Mad Lib is a brief one-page story with words left blank for the readers to fill in following the specific part of speech the directions call for. A typical example titled "Page from a Psychiatrist's Notebook" begins as follows:

> This is the case history of _____ (person in room), who is suffering from a/an _____ (noun) complex. He/She also has abnormal fears of _____ (plural noun) and _____ (plural noun).... (Price & Stern, 1991, n.p.)

Mad Libs are fun to play in class and offer adults a nonthreatening way of exploring different parts of speech. (Once again, this is especially helpful for ELLs.) At times I have also had students compose their own Mad Libs and then play them with others in class or at home.

Responding to a British government-funded study that found formal grammar instruction is ineffective in helping students learn how to become competent writers and lovers of language, Philip Pullman, the noted novelist and modern fantasy writer, observed,

> If teachers knew something about the joy of *fooling about with words* [italics added], their pupils would write with much greater fluency and effectiveness. Teachers and pupils alike would see that the only reason for writing is to produce something true and beautiful; that they were on the same side, with the teacher as mentor, as editor, not as instructor and measurer, critic and judge. (2005, n.p.)

Although Pullman was writing about children and young adults, the same thing applies to adult literacy instructors and students—perhaps even more so. If you're tempted to pass out the grammar workbook pages to your students, stop and think first about the value of "fooling about with words."

LOOK FOR COMMON MISTAKES

Obviously, the most practical and productive thing to do is to keep a record of the difficulties with grammar and punctuation that your students have in common. Typically you will find that more than one person—indeed, many—will struggle with the same things. You can then build specific lessons around those particular needs. This is very different from using an exercise from a workbook or "canned" curriculum with all students, whether they need it or not. Moreover, simply asking adults what they need or what they're confused about with regard to grammar and punctuation will help you target minilessons and activities for individual students. This is especially important for ELLs who might come from many different language backgrounds with varying levels of education and proficiency in English.

Final Thoughts

SOME YEARS AGO after working every week with a woman in an adult basic education class, I wrote a poem about our experiences together. I was not the regular teacher but instead was the "college prof" who came weekly to write with the students. This particular woman inspired me with her determination and sheer endurance. She worked part-time as a cleaning woman in a large hotel downtown, took care of her children as a single parent, and worried (rightly so) about the violence that plagued her community. She had dropped out of school when she became pregnant and carried with her all of the negative baggage from her experiences as a special education student in the elementary and secondary grades. She had little confidence in her own literacy abilities although they were not minimal. After writing short prose pieces and different kinds of poems with the students for some weeks, I asked the students to try a poem on their own at home. The following week this woman shyly showed me a little poem she wrote about her hopes for her children and her concerns for their safety. Her poem served as inspiration for mine.

"Dancing in the Adult Literacy Class"

"I wrote a poem," she whispered,
"You know, like you asked us.
It's about my babies,
And how I need more than part-time."
"May I see it?"
She opened her blue binder
Covered with stickers of animals—
It must have been one of her kid's—
And slipped from between the worksheets
A single piece of wide-ruled paper.
"It's not too good I think."
Her careful pencil strokes
Swirled in a stiff-legged dance
Of misspellings, missed grammar,
And freedom from punctuation.
I read it silently, and again,
Trying to enter the movement
Of her skipping language.

I asked her to show me
The steps I couldn't follow;
Then I read it aloud, tentatively,
Slowly moving to the rhythms
And motions of her words.
I read it again, sure now
Of all that the poem carried.
And again, this time with her
Joining me in counterpoint,
Maid's fingers tracking each word.
It was in our telling together
That her words reflected the grace
Hidden in the flurry of print:
Lines rose and shone in beauty,
Longing, and a mother's hope:
"I pray for my children,
Going out to school
Coming home from school..."
On the urban streets of hopelessness.
"That don't sound like me!"
She grinned and shook her head
In bafflement and wonder.
"It sounds like, you know,
Somebody who could really write,
You know, sort of like a poet."
And then we danced it again.

It was her words, her poetry, her art, that brought us together in the dance. By making something beautiful with language and by generously sharing it with me she honored literacy and demonstrated its power to help us shape our worlds in many different ways. She became one of my handful of touchstones to whom I refer whenever I'm reading and writing with students of any age, whether they might be elementary children, adolescents in alternative learning centers, undergraduate students, elders in community centers, or adults in basic skills programs. This book and all of the ideas and activities in it are grounded in my belief in the dance of language and in the music of what happens in our daily lives.

References

Alderson, D. (1996). *Talking back to poems: A working guide for the aspiring poet*. Berkeley, CA: Celestial Arts Publishing.

Allington, R.L. (2005). *What really matters for struggling readers: Designing research-based programs* (2nd ed.). Boston: Allyn & Bacon.

Asher, J.J. (1977). *Learning another language through actions: The complete teacher's guidebook*. Los Gatos, CA: Sky Oaks Productions.

Auerbach, E.R. (1992). *Making meaning, making change: Participatory curriculum for adult ESL literacy*. Washington, DC: Center for Applied Linguistics.

Auerbach, E.R. (1999, December). The power of writing, the writing of power: Approaches to ESOL writing instruction. *Focus on Basics: Connecting Research & Practice, 3*(Issue D). Retrieved June 17, 2006, from www.ncsall.net/?id=341

Bailey, K.M. (2006). Issues in teaching speaking skills to adult ESOL learners. In J. Comings, B. Garner, & C. Smith (Eds.), *Review of adult learning and literacy* (Vol. 6, pp. 113–164). Mahwah, NJ: Erlbaum.

Barton, D., & Hamilton, M. (1998). *Local literacies: Reading and writing in one community*. London: Routledge.

Belfiore, M.E., Defoe, T.A., Folinsbee, S., Hunter, J., & Jackson, N.S. (2004). *Reading work: Literacies in the new workplace*. Mahwah, NJ: Erlbaum.

Berthoff, A.E. (1981). *The making of meaning: Metaphors, models, and maxims for writing teachers*. Portsmouth, NH: Boynton/Cook.

Brandt, D. (2001). *Literacy in American lives*. New York: Cambridge University Press.

Britton, J. (1982). *Prospect and retrospect: Selected essays of James Britton*. (G.M. Pradl, Ed.) Portsmouth, NH: Boynton/Cook.

Brown, C.S. (1988). *Like it was: A complete guide to writing oral history*. New York: Teachers & Writers Collaborative.

Brown, R.M. (1988). Marks and squiggles. *Christianity and Crisis, 48*, 333–334.

Bruner, J. (1962). *On knowing: Essays for the left hand*. Cambridge, MA: Harvard University Press.

Bui, T. (1999, December). How I wish I was taught to write. *Focus on Basics: Connecting Research & Practice, 3*(Issue D). Retrieved June 24, 2006, from www.ncsall.net/?id=340

Campbell, D. (1997). *The Mozart effect: Tapping the power of music to heal the body, strengthen the mind, and unlock the creative spirit*. New York: Avon.

Cassidy, J., Garcia, R., Tejeda-Delgado, C., Garrett, S.D., Martinez-Garcia, C., & Hinojosa, R.V. (2004). A learner-centered family literacy project for Latino parents and caregivers. *Journal of Adolescent & Adult Literacy, 47*(6), 478–488.

Chiseri-Strater, E. (1994). World travelling: Enlarging our understanding of nonmainstream literacies. In B.J. Moss (Ed.), *Literacy across communities* (pp. 179–186). Cresskill, NJ: Hampton Press.

Collignon, F.F. (1994). From "paj ntaub" to paragraphs: Perspectives on Hmong processes of composing. In V. John-Steiner, C.P. Panofsky, & L.W. Smith (Eds.), *Sociocultural approaches to language and literacy: An interactionist perspective* (pp. 331–346). New York: Cambridge University Press.

Coustan, T. (2004). Learning English through movement: Making sentences. In J. Viens & S. Kallenbach, *Multiple intelligences and adult literacy: A sourcebook for practitioners* (p. 89). New York: Teachers College Press.

Covington, D. (1994). Snake handling and redemption. *The Georgia Review, XLVIII*(4), 667–692.

Crandall, J., & Peyton, J.K., (Eds.). (1993). *Approaches to adult ESL instruction*. Washington, DC: Center for Applied Linguistics; McHenry, IL: Delta Systems.

D'Annunzio, A. (1994). A nondirective combinatory model in an adult ESL program. In M.C. Radencich (Ed.), *Adult literacy: A compendium of articles from the* Journal of Reading (pp. 157–162). Newark, DE: International Reading Association.

Davies, R. (1996). *The merry heart: Reflections on reading, writing, and the world of books*. New York: Viking Penguin.

Demetrion, G. (2005). *Conflicting paradigms in adult literacy education: In quest of a U.S. democratic politics of literacy*. Mahwah, NJ: Erlbaum.

Dewey, J. (1934). *Art as experience*. New York: Capricorn Books.

Drago-Severson, E. (2004). *Becoming adult learners: Principles and practices for effective development*. New York: Teachers College Press.

Ewald, W. (2002). *I wanna take me a picture: Teaching photography and writing to children*. Boston: Center for Documentary Studies/Beacon Press.

Fagan, W.T. (1998). *Literacy for living: A study of literacy and cultural context in rural Canadian communities*. St. John's, NL: Memorial University of Newfoundland, ISER Books.

Farr, M. (1994). En los dos idiomas: Literacy practices among Chicago Mexicanos. In B.J. Moss (Ed.), *Literacy across communities* (pp. 9–47). Cresskill, NJ: Hampton Press.

Freire, P. (1970). *Pedagogy of the oppressed*. New York: Seabury Press.

Gee, J.P. (2008). *Social linguistics and literacies: Ideology in discourses* (3rd ed.). New York: Routledge.

Gordon, K.E. (1984). *The transitive vampire: A handbook of grammar for the innocent, the eager, and the doomed*. New York: Times Books.

Gordon, K.E. (1993). *The deluxe transitive vampire: The ultimate handbook of grammar for the innocent, the eager, and the doomed*. New York: Pantheon Books.

Graff, H.J. (1995). *The labyrinths of literacy: Reflections on literacy past and present*. (Rev. ed.) Pittsburgh: University of Pittsburgh Press.

Graham, C. (1978). *Jazz chants: Rhythms of American English for students of English as a second language*. New York: Oxford University Press.

Hall, D. (1993). *Poetry: The unsayable said*. Port Townsend, WA: Copper Canyon Press.

Hillman, J. (1996). *The soul's code: In search of character and calling*. New York: Random House.

Hillman, J. (1999). *The force of character: And the lasting life*. New York: Random House.

Horsman, J. (1990). *Something in my mind besides the everyday: Women and literacy*. Toronto: Women's Press.

Howarth, K. (1998). *Oral history*. Stroud, England: Sutton.

Hull, G. (1999). Literacy and labeling. *Journal of Adolescent & Adult Literacy, 42*(7), 540–544.

Isay, D. (2007). *Listening is an act of love: A celebration of American life from the StoryCorps project*. New York: Penguin.

Kahn, A. (2002). *A love supreme: The creation of John Coltrane's classic album*. London: Granta Books.

Kazemek, C., & Kazemek, F.E. (1992). Systems theory: A way of looking at adult literacy education. *Convergence, 25*(3), 5–15.

Kazemek, F.E. (1991). "In ignorance to view a small portion and think that all": The false promise of job literacy. *Journal of Education, 173*(1), 51–64.

Kazemek, F.E. (1992). Looking at adult literacy obliquely: Poetry, stories, imagination, metaphor, and gossip. *Adult Basic Education, 2*(3), 144–160.

Kazemek, F.E. (1998). O public road...you express me better than I can express myself. In H. Woodrow & C. McGrath (Eds.), *Wayfaring: Journeys in language and culture* (pp. 54–64). St. John's, NL: Harrish Press.

Kazemek, F.E. (1999a). "A gathering of individuals": A longitudinal study of a writing workshop for older adults. *Adult Basic Education, 9*(1), 3–20.

Kazemek, F.E. (1999b). Mary's story: Reflections on literacy. *Journal of Adolescent & Adult Literacy, 42*(8), 604–609.

Kazemek, F.E. (2002a). *Exploring our lives: A writing handbook for senior adults*. Santa Monica, CA: Santa Monica Press.

Kazemek, F.E. (2002b). I know lots of people have those thoughts, they just do. *Journal of Adolescent & Adult Literacy, 45*(5), 378–380.

Kazemek, F.E. (2002c). Monk, Bird, 'Trane, and Miles: Jazz in the English language arts program. *ALAN Review, 29*(3), 45–49.

Kazemek, F.E. (2004). Living a literate life. *Journal of Adolescent & Adult Literacy, 47*(6), 448–452.

Kazemek, F.E., & Rigg, P. (1995). *Enriching our lives: Poetry lessons for adult literacy teachers and tutors*. Newark, DE: International Reading Association.

Kazemek, F.E., & Rigg, P. (1997). "...the sense of soul...goes hand in hand with an aesthetic response": Art in adult literacy education. *Adult Basic Education, 7*(3), 131–144.

Key, D. (1998). *Literacy shutdown: Stories of six American women*. Newark, DE: International Reading Association.

Koch, K. (1970). *Wishes, lies, and dreams: Teaching children to write poetry*. New York: Random House.

Koch, K. (1977). *I never told anybody: Teaching poetry writing in a nursing home*. New York: Random House.

Krashen, S.D. (1982). *Principles and practice in second language acquisition*. New York: Pergamon Press.

Krashen, S.D. (2004). *The power of reading: Insights from the research* (2nd ed.). Portsmouth, NH: Heinemann.

Leavitt, H.D., & Sohn, D.A. (1964). *Stop, look, and write! Effective writing through pictures*. New York: Bantam Pathfinder Editions.

McLuhan, M. (1994). *Understanding media: The extensions of man*. Cambridge, MA: MIT Press.

Millar, R. (2007). Diagnostic assessment. In P. Campbell (Ed.), *Measures of success: Assessment and accountability in adult basic education* (pp. 69–91). Edmonton, AB: Grass Roots Press.

Mohr, K.A.J. (1994). Variations on a theme: Using thematically framed language experience activities for English as a second language (ESL) instruction. In O.G. Nelson & W.M. Linek (Eds.), *Practical classroom applications of language experience: Looking back, looking forward* (pp. 237–247). Boston: Allyn & Bacon.

Nagy, W.E. (1988). *Teaching vocabulary to improve reading comprehension*. Washington, DC: ERIC Clearinghouse on Reading and Communication Skills.

Nash, A., Cason, A., Rhum, M., McGrail, L., & Gomez-Sanford, R. (1992). *Talking shop: A curriculum sourcebook for participatory adult ESL*. Washington, DC: Center for Applied Linguistics; McHenry, IL: Delta Systems.

National Council of Teachers of English ELL Task Force. (2006). *NCTE position paper on the role of English teachers in educating English language learners (ELLs)*. Urbana, IL: National Council of Teachers of English. Retrieved March 20, 2008, from www.ncte.org/about/over/positions/category/div/124545.htm

Padak, N.D., & Bardine, B.A. (2004). Engaging readers and writers in adult education contexts. *Journal of Adolescent & Adult Literacy, 48*(2), 126–137. doi:10.1598/JAAL.48.2.4

Pates, A., & Evans, M. (1994). Writing workshops: An experience from British adult literacy. In M.C. Radencich (Ed.), *Adult literacy: A compendium of articles from the* Journal of Reading (pp. 143–149). Newark, DE: International Reading Association.

Peyton, J.K. (1993). Listening to students' voices: Publishing students' writing for other students to read. In J. Crandall & J.K. Peyton (Eds.), *Approaches to adult ESL literacy instruction* (pp. 59–73). McHenry, IL: Center for Applied Linguistics.

Pullman, P. (2005). Common sense has much to learn from moonshine. *Guardian Unlimited*. Retrieved January 25, 2005, from books.guardian.co.uk/news/articles/0,6109,1396252,00.html

Purcell-Gates, V. (1995). *Other people's words: The cycle of low literacy*. Cambridge, MA: Harvard University Press.

Purcell-Gates, V., Degener, S.C., Jacobson, E., & Soler, M. (2002). Impact of authentic adult literacy instruction on adult literacy practices. *Reading Research Quarterly, 37*(1), 70–92. doi:10.1598/RRQ.37.1.3

Purcell-Gates, V., Jacobson, E., & Degener, S. (2004). *Print literacy development: Uniting cognitive and social practice theories*. Cambridge, MA: Harvard University Press.

Purcell-Gates, V., & Waterman, R. (2000). *Now we read, we see, we speak: Portrait of literacy development in an adult Freirean-based class*. Mahwah, NJ: Erlbaum.

Rigg, P., & Kazemek, F.E. (1993). Whole language in adult literacy education. In J. Crandall & J.K. Peyton (Eds.), *Approaches to adult ESL literacy instruction* (pp. 35–46). McHenry, IL: Center for Applied Linguistics.

Rogers, R. (2004). Storied selves: A critical discourse analysis of adult learners' literate lives. *Reading Research Quarterly, 39*(3), 272–305. doi:10.1598/RRQ.39.3.2

Rosenblatt, L.M. (1978). *The reader, the text, the poem: The transactional theory of the literary work*. Carbondale: Southern Illinois University Press.

Sanders, B. (1994). *A is for ox: Violence, electronic media, and the silencing of the written word*. New York: Pantheon Books.

Sanders, S.R. (1997). The power of stories. *The Georgia Review, 51*(1), 113–126.

Schank, R.C. (1990). *Tell me a story: A new look at real and artificial memory*. New York: Scribner.

Smith, L. (1996, June 28). Given tools, they work the language [Opinion]. The *New York Times*. Retrieved March 20, 2008, from query.nytimes.com/gst/fullpage.html?res=9507EED81239F93BA15755C0A960958260&sec=&spon=&pagewanted=1

Soifer, R., Irwin, M.E., Crumrine, B.M., Honzaki, E., Simmons, B.K., & Young, D.L. (1990). *The complete theory-to-practice handbook of adult literacy: Curriculum design and teaching approaches*. New York: Teachers College Press.

Sontag, S. (1977). *On photography*. New York: Picador/Farrar, Straus and Giroux.

Stories of Ageing Project. (1999). *We're not nice little old ladies*. Melbourne, Australia: University of Melbourne.

Strunk, W., Jr., & White, E.B. (1979). *The elements of style* (3rd ed.). New York: Macmillan.

Stuckey, J.E. (1991). *The violence of literacy*. Portsmouth, NH: Boynton/Cook.

Taylor, M.C. (2006). Informal adult learning and everyday literacy practices. *Journal of Adolescent & Adult Literacy, 49*(6), 500–509. doi:10.1598/JAAL.49.6.5

Terkel, S. (1980). *American dreams: Lost and found*. New York: Pantheon Books.

Terkel, S. (2003). *Hope dies last: Keeping the faith in difficult times*. New York: The New Press.

Tisdell, E.J. (1999). The spiritual dimension of adult development. In M.C. Clark & R.S. Caffarella (Eds.), *An update on adult development theory: New ways of thinking about the life course* (New Directions for Adult and Continuing Education No. 84, pp. 87–96). San Francisco: Jossey-Bass.

Twain, M. (1888). Letter to George Bainton, 10/15/1888. Retrieved April 24, 2008, from www.twainquotes.com/Lightning.html

Velazquez, L.C. (1996). Voices from the fields: Community-based migrant education. In P.A. Sissel (Ed.), *A community-based approach to literacy programs: Taking learners' lives into account* (New Directions for Adult and Continuing Education No. 70, pp. 27–35). San Francisco: Jossey-Bass.

Viens, J., & Kallenbach, S. (2004). *Multiple intelligences and adult literacy: A sourcebook for practitioners*. New York: Teachers College Press.

Vygotsky, L.S. (1978). *Mind in society: The development of higher psychological processes* (M. Cole, V. John-Steiner, S. Scribner, & E. Souberman, Eds. & Trans.). Cambridge, MA: Harvard University Press.

Weibel, M.C. (1996). *Choosing & using books with adult new readers*. New York: Neal-Schuman.

Weiner, E.J. (2005/2006). Keeping adults behind: Adult literacy education in the age of official reading regimes. *Journal of Adolescent & Adult Literacy, 49*(4), 286–301. doi:10.1598/JAAL.49.4.3

Weinstein-Shr, G. (1994). From mountaintops to city streets: Literacy in Philadelphia's Hmong community. In B.J. Moss (Ed.), *Literacy across communities* (pp. 49–83). Cresskill, NJ: Hampton Press.

Wigginton, E. (Ed.). (1972). *The Foxfire book*. Garden City, NY: Anchor Books.

Woodrow, H., & Kazemek, F.E. (2001). Oral histories in the adult literacy program. *NALD Networks, 6*(1), 3.

LITERATURE AND MUSIC CITED

Berry, W. (1998). "1994: VII (I would not have been a poet)." In *A timbered choir: The Sabbath poems 1979–1997* (p. 182). Washington, DC: Counterpoint.

Blake, W. (1988). "The fly." In D.V. Erdman (Ed.), *The complete poetry & prose of William Blake* (pp. 23–24). New York: Doubleday.

Cohen, L., & Matisse, H. (1996). *Dance me to the end of love*. New York: Welcome Books.

cummings, e.e., & Chagall, M. (1995). *May I feel said he*. New York: Welcome Books.

Dickinson, E. (1960). *The complete poems of Emily Dickinson*. Boston: Little, Brown.

Dylan, B. (2004). *Chronicles, volume one*. New York: Simon & Schuster.

Farrell, K. (1990). *Art & love: An illustrated anthology of love poetry*. New York: Metropolitan Museum of Art; Boston: Bulfinch Press.

Farrell, K. (1999). *Time's river: The voyage of life in art and poetry*. Washington, DC: National Gallery of Art; Boston: Little, Brown.

Frost, R. (1969). Fire and ice. In E.C. Lathem (Ed.), *The poetry of Robert Frost* (p. 220). Austin, TX: Holt, Rinehart and Winston.

Guthrie, W. (1965). *Born to win*. New York: Macmillan.

Harburg, E.Y., & Parrish, M. (2000). *Over the rainbow*. New York: Welcome Books.

Hemingway, E. (1987). The big two-hearted river: Part I. In *The complete short stories of Ernest Hemingway* (pp. 163–169). New York: Scribner.

Koch, K., & Farrell, K. (1985). *Talking to the sun: An illustrated anthology of poems for young people*. New York: Henry Holt.

Moss, S. (Ed.). (1998). *The world's shortest stories: Murder. Love. Horror. Suspense. All this and much more in the most amazing short stories ever written—each one just 55 words long!* Philadelphia: Running Press Books.

Moyers, B. (1995). *The language of life: A festival of poets*. New York: Doubleday.

Parks, S.L. (2006). *365 days/365 plays*. New York: Theatre Communications Group.

Price, R., & Stern, L. (1991). *Wacky mad libs V*. New York: Scholastic.

Sandburg, C. (1958). *Early moon*. New York: Harcourt Brace Jovanovich.

Sandburg, C. (1970). The people, yes. In *The complete poems of Carl Sandburg* (p. 492). New York: Harcourt Brace Jovanovich.

Schwartz, A. (2006). *Scary stories to tell in the dark*. New York: HarperTrophy.

Shakespeare, W. (1963). Sonnet 111. In *All the love poems of Shakespeare* (pp. 108–109). Secaucus, NJ: Citadel Press.

Shange, N., & Bearden, R. (1994). *i live in music*. New York: Welcome Books.

Shepard, A. (2002). *The Calabash kids: A tale of Tanzania* [Readers Theatre edition]. Retrieved April 23, 2008, from www.aaronshep.com/rt/RTE11.html

Smith, B. (2005). Gulf coast blues. On *Greatest hits* [CD]. Minneapolis, MN: Fabulous.

Stafford, W. (1998). What's in my journal. In *The way it is: New & selected poems* (p. 248). St. Paul, MN: Graywolf Press.

Sting, & Picasso, P. (1998). *Shape of my heart*. New York: Welcome Books.

Szymborska, W. (1993). *View with a grain of sand: Selected poems* (S. Baranczak & C. Cavanagh, Trans.). New York: Harcourt Brace & Company.

The Holy Bible. King James Version. (1971). Nashville, TN: Gideons International.

The psalms: The book of praises with commentary by Kathleen Norris. (1997). New York: Riverhead Books.

Thomas, J., Thomas, D., & Hazuka, T. (1992). *Flash fiction: Very short stories*. New York: W.W. Norton.

Thomas, R.S. (1997). *Autobiographies*. London: J.M. Dent.

Vallejo, C. (1978). Nomina de huesos/Payroll of bones. In *César Vallejo: The complete posthumous poems* (C. Eshleman & J.R. Barcia, Trans.; pp. 2–3). Berkeley: University of California Press.

Volkov, S. (1998). *Conversations with Joseph Brodsky: A poet's journey through the twentieth century*. New York: The Free Press.

Walsh, J.B., & Sherman, T. (1915). *The Broadway blues*. Retrieved April 23, 2008, from www.jumbojimbo .com/lyrics.php?songid=4582

Welty, E. (1984). *One writer's beginnings*. Cambridge, MA: Harvard University Press.

Whitman, W. (1983). *Leaves of grass: The 1892 edition*. New York: Bantam Books.

Williams, C. (1923). *Gulf coast blues*. Retrieved April 23, 2008, from www.lyricstime.com/bessie-smith -gulf-coast-blues-lyrics.html

Williams, W.C. (1963). *Paterson*. New York: New Directions.

Williams, W.C. (1986a). The great figure. In A.W. Litz & C. MacGowan (Eds.), *Collected poems: 1909–1939, Volume I* (p. 174). New York: New Directions.

Williams, W.C. (1986b). Spring and all. In A.W. Litz & C. MacGowan (Eds.), *Collected poems: 1909–1939, Volume I* (pp. 175–236). New York: New Directions.

Williams, W.C. (1986c). This is just to say. In A.W. Litz & C. MacGowan (Eds.), *Collected poems: 1909–1939, Volume I* (p. 372). New York: New Directions.

Williams, W.C. (1988a). Detail (Doc, I bin). In C. MacGowan (Ed.), *Collected poems 1939–1962, Volume II* (pp. 20–21). New York: New Directions.

Williams, W.C. (1988b). Detail (Hey!). In C. MacGowan (Ed.), *Collected poems 1939–1962, Volume II* (p. 19). New York: New Directions.

Williams, W.C. (1988c). The corn harvest. In C. MacGowan (Ed.), *Collected poems 1939–1962, Volume II* (pp. 389–390). New York: New Directions.

Index

Page numbers in *italics* indicate figures.

Notes

Notes

Notes

Notes